VOLUME NINETY FOUR

ADVANCES IN
COMPUTERS

VOLUME NINETY FOUR

ADVANCES IN
COMPUTERS

Edited by

ALI HURSON
Department of Computer Science
Missouri University of Science and Technology
325 Computer Science Building
Rolla, MO 65409-0350
USA
Email: hurson@mst.edu

AMSTERDAM • BOSTON • HEIDELBERG • LONDON
NEW YORK • OXFORD • PARIS • SAN DIEGO
SAN FRANCISCO • SINGAPORE • SYDNEY • TOKYO
Academic Press is an imprint of Elsevier

ELSEVIER

Academic Press is an imprint of Elsevier
225 Wyman Street, Waltham, MA 02451, USA
525 B Street, Suite 1800, San Diego, CA 92101-4495, USA
The Boulevard, Langford Lane, Kidlington, Oxford, OX51GB, UK
32, Jamestown Road, London NW1 7BY, UK

First edition 2014

Library of Congress Cataloging-in-Publication Data
A catalog record for this book is available from the Library of Congress

British Library Cataloguing-in-Publication Data
A catalogue record for this book is available from the British Library

ISBN: 978-0-12-800161-5
ISSN: 0065-2458

For information on all Academic Press publications
visit our web site at store.elsevier.com

Working together
to grow libraries in
developing countries

www.elsevier.com • www.bookaid.org

CONTENTS

PREFACE

Traditionally, *Advances in Computers*, the oldest series to chronicle the rapid evolution of computing, annually publishes several volumes, each typically comprised of four to eight chapters, describing new developments in the theory and applications of computing. The theme of this 94th volume is inspired by the advances in information technology. Within the spectrum of information technology, this volume touches several issues in security and software evolution. The volume is a collection of four chapters that were solicited from authorities in the field, each of whom brings to bear a unique perspective on the topic.

In Chapter 1, "Comparison of Security Models: Attack Graphs Versus Petri Nets," White and Sedigh articulate needs for modeling of system and information security in order to facilitate formal representation and analysis of security to identify and address the vulnerabilities. Both static and dynamic security models exemplified by attach graphs and Petri nets are discussed. This discussion is also enhanced by extending the models to capture nondeterministic behavior. The aforementioned models are analyzed based on accuracy and potential for decision support. Finally, they concluded that dynamic models such as Petri nets are more powerful than their static counterparts (i.e., attack graphs).

In Chapter 2, "A Survey on Zero-Knowledge Proofs," Feng and McMillin defined "zero-knowledge proofs (ZKPs)" as interactive protocols where one party (i.e., prover) can convince the other party (i.e., verifier) that some assertion is true without revealing anything other than the fact that the assertion being proven is true. The property of being convincing and yielding nothing except the assertion is valid making ZKPs very powerful tools for the design of secure cryptographic protocols. The zero-knowledge proofs have been used in many applications such as identity verification, authentication, key exchange, and enforcing the honest behavior while maintaining privacy. In this chapter, the concept of the zero-knowledge proofs has been extensively surveyed by the authors.

The concept of "Similarity of Private Keyword Search over Encrypted Document Collection" is the main theme of Chapter 3. Outsourcing data to the "cloud" has numerous advantages such as cost effectiveness, flexibility, and off-loading of administrative overhead. These advantages come at the expense of data owner's loss of control over the data (the cloud provider becomes a third-party service provider). Data encryption is a common practice to overcome this difficulty and protect the confidentiality of the outsourced data from the third-party provider. However, encryption of data adds another layer of complexity and challenges for query processing over encrypted data without ever decrypting it. Private keyword search allows a user to search for the most similar objects to his/her request over encrypted data without nothing be leaked beyond the search and access patterns. Consequently, the document collection, the user query, and the retrieved results are encrypted so that the server who processes this keyword search does not learn any information regarding the original documents and the content of a user's query. The chapter presents a comprehensive survey on the existing private keyword search techniques.

Finally, in Chapter 4, "Multiobjective Optimization for Software Refactoring and Evolution," Ouni *et al.* address refactoring as a technique to improve design structure while preserving the external behavior of software systems after its delivery. Refactoring should be of interest to software designers since it eases the software maintenance. As noted by the article, in general, refactoring is performed in two main steps: (1) detection of code fragments corresponding to design defects (i.e., design features that adversely affect the development of software) that need to be improved or fixed and (2) identification of refactoring solutions to improve or fix the defects identified in the first step. A multiobjective search-based approach is used to find the optimal sequence of refactoring operations that improve the software quality by minimizing the number of detected defects. In short, this article proposes a novel approach for automating the detection and correction of design defects and studying the impact of refactoring on design defects during software evolution.

I hope that you find these articles of interest and useful in your teaching, research, and other professional activities. I welcome feedback on the volume and suggestions for topics for future volumes.

ALI R. HURSON
Missouri University of Science and Technology,
Rolla, MO, USA

CHAPTER ONE

Comparison of Security Models: Attack Graphs Versus Petri Nets

Steven C. White, Sahra Sedigh Sarvestani

Department of Electrical and Computer Engineering, Missouri University of Science and Technology, Rolla, Missouri, USA

Contents

Abstract

Modeling of system and information security aims to facilitate formal representation and analysis of security, where vulnerabilities are identified and addressed. This chapter discusses the two categories of static and dynamic security models, as exemplified by attack graphs and Petri nets, respectively. Also discussed is the significant enhancement that results from extending these models to capture nondeterministic behavior, in stochastic attack graphs and stochastic Petri nets, respectively. The models are evaluated and compared with respect to (i) accuracy and (ii) potential for decision support, and Petri nets are found to be superior to attack graphs in both criteria.

Advances in Computers, Volume 94
ISSN 0065-2458
http://dx.doi.org/10.1016/B978-0-12-800161-5.00001-3

LIST OF ABBREVIATIONS
BDMP Boolean logic-driven Markov process
CTMC Continuous-time Markov chain
MDP Markov decision process
pmf Probability mass function
UML Universal markup language

1. INTRODUCTION

Protection of the vast amount of data collected, stored, and transmitted in today's computer systems is a critically important, yet increasingly challenging task. One means of verifying this protection is through the use of security models that serve as useful abstractions. Despite several decades of effort by academia and industry, existing models for the security of information systems have several limitations. The first is their complexity—an impediment to visualization and manipulation of the model. Limiting this complexity leads to a second limitation: inaccuracy. Research is needed to develop modeling techniques that decompose a complex information system into manageable parts, model each part, and aggregate the resulting information into a useful system-level model.

Security models can be divided into two major categories—*static* and *dynamic*—based on whether they include a time dimension [1]. The advantages of the static models are readability and ease of creation and interpretation of results. The major drawback of static models is that they capture states of the system but do not show interactions of the system states over time. This drawback limits their modeling power and ability to provide quantifiable results. A common static model is the attack tree or attack graph. Variations of attack trees include threat trees, vulnerability trees, and defense trees [1–4]. All of these models are relatively simple to create and interpret.

Dynamic models, which are capable of capturing changes in the system over time, are the second major category. Models in this category include state space or stochastic state-space models [5], Boolean logic-driven Markov processes [1], and Petri nets. The fundamental advantage of dynamic models is the ability to capture changes and interactions as the system and/or attacks evolve over time. The drawbacks are complexity, readability, and scalability—state-space explosion can occur rather quickly for a complex system, rendering exhaustive analysis infeasible.

The remainder of this chapter includes three sections on models, analysis techniques, and conclusions, respectively. Section 2, on models, introduces the two broad categories of security models—static and dynamic, with emphasis on attack graphs from the former category and Petri nets from the latter. In Sections 3 and 4, we describe and compare the use of attack graphs and Petri nets in analysis of security. We also illustrate the application of these models to a simple computer system, which is modeled with an attack graph, a classic Petri net, a stochastic attack graph, and finally a stochastic Petri net. Two attributes of each model are emphasized: accuracy and potential for decision support. Section 5 concludes the chapter by highlighting the result of comparing these models—which stochastic Petri nets outperform attack graphs in both accuracy and decision power.

2. STATIC AND DYNAMIC SECURITY MODELS

In surveying existing security models, we have selected attack graphs as a representative static modeling technique to be compared with a representative dynamic technique—Petri nets. The selection of attack graphs was due to their effectiveness in visualization. Petri nets share this feature, hence their selection over other dynamic modeling techniques such as state model diagrams, state charts, Boolean logic–driven Markov processes (BDMPs), and attack–response graphs. Each of these competing models has advantages and disadvantages. State model diagrams and state charts have advantages of maturity in the area of software development. As outlined in Ref.[6], software development uses the Unified Modeling Language, which can be extended to modeling of security. Drawbacks of state models include potential for state-space explosion and the inability to capture details or low-level descriptions of complex systems. BDMP evolved from the dependability domain into security modeling. As stated in Ref.[7], BDMPs provide quantification capabilities while balancing readability, scalability, and modeling power. Unlike static models, BDMP and other dynamic models allow time-domain analysis and dynamic characterization of an attack. As a drawback, BDMPs are vulnerable to state-space explosion.

2.1 Attack Graphs

Threat trees, attack trees, and attack graphs first appeared in computer security literature in the mid- to late-1990s [8]. These techniques are useful in the visualization of attacks and vulnerabilities. Attack graphs aim to represent all possible sequences of actions that can lead to successful compromise of a system by a given attacker. The nodes represent actions taken; the arcs

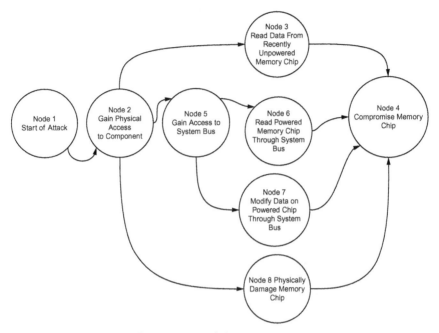

Figure 1.1 Attack graph of a memory exploit.

show causality among these actions. One or more actions can serve as the precondition(s) for a different action. Figure 1.1 is an example of simple attack graph used to model the physical security exploits used to compromise a memory chip. This graph is provided as a simplistic example in order to focus on the analysis of an attack graph. The graph does not contain all possible actions and is composed of a single goal, with four paths of attack. In this example, all nodes are OR nodes; that is, no action has more than one other action as a required precondition. As such, the attacker has multiple paths to reach the goal. The model illustrates the vulnerabilities exploited in order to successfully reach the goal—successful compromise of the system.

This example shows the ease with which an attack tree can be constructed—vulnerabilities are enumerated, corresponding exploits are represented as nodes, and arcs between the nodes represented the directed path that connects the initial action to the final goal. Attack graphs can be manually or automatically generated; several tools exist for the latter. Reference [9] is considered a seminal study on their automated generation. One of the positives of this approach is that it facilitates identification and emphasis of critical vulnerabilities. One of the drawbacks of early attack graphs was the inability to represent cost or nondeterminism. More recent representations include attributes such as cost, time, skill level, or probability as attributes of the nodes or arcs of the graph. Analysis that considers these attributes provides additional information about possible attacks. In our example, we could add a "difficulty" attribute for the exploit represented by each node. This extension gives added value to the attack graph and facilitates its use in decision support for mitigation of vulnerabilities. Attack graphs have been used with other analysis methods to determine which approach to use to decrease the likelihood of an attack [10]. In short, the fundamental benefit of attack graphs is the facilitation of brainstorming on and visualization of the steps involved in compromising a system. The fundamental drawback of attack graphs is their inability to incorporate properties of the system or environment.

2.2 Stochastic Attack Graphs

In the first part of this section, attack graphs were discussed and a simple attack graph was presented and analyzed. In the second part, in preparation for comparison of stochastic modeling of attack graphs and Petri nets, the example of using attack graphs will be extended to incorporate nondeterminism.

In examining published research, we found very few studies where stochastic processes were considered in generation of attack graphs. Two noteworthy studies on the topic are Refs. [11,12]. The first paper outlines how to determine the risk level and the stochastic shortest path in order to identify the optimal path of intrusion. The paper investigates two different stages of the system life cycle—network design and network defense. The advantage of this approach over classical attack graphs is the ability to determine the probability that a host will be compromised. The underlying analysis approach is to use Markov decision models to determine the probability of compromise and shortest exploit path.

Based on this approach, we illustrate the stochastic counterpart of the attack graph of Fig. 1.1. Figure 1.2 depicts the stochastic attack graph from which the stochastic Markov decision process (MDP) graph is derived, where circles represent states, trapezoids represent prerequisite nodes, and triangles represent vulnerability instance nodes.

The second noteworthy paper on stochastic attack graphs [12] uses Petri nets to enhance the effectiveness of attack graphs. The idea is to use stochastic Petri nets to model the system as it is defined by the attack graph. This is similar to the approach we present in Section 4.2, where we discuss, in terms of modeling and decision power, the advantages of utilizing Petri nets instead of attack graphs.

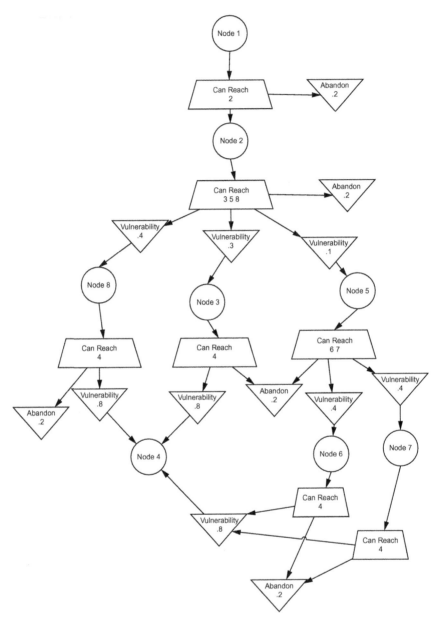

Figure 1.2 Stochastic attack graph of a memory exploit.

2.3 Petri Nets

A Petri net is a graphical abstraction used to represent concurrent interactions among multiple components of a system. More specifically, a Petri net is a directed bipartite graph composed of nodes that represent transitions, places that represent preconditions, and directed arcs that associate places and transitions. Depending on the direction of the arc, a place may be denoted as an input place (precondition) or a output place (postcondition) for a transition with which it is associated. A Petri net is considered *marked* when tokens are assigned to places within the graph [13,14]. A detailed example is provided in Section 4.

Formally, a marked Petri net is a tuple, $PN = (P, T, F, W, M)$, where:

1. $P = (p_1, p_2, \ldots, p_n)$ is a finite set of places (conditions).
2. $M = (m_1, m_2, \ldots, m_n)$ is a finite set of nonnegative integers denoting the marking of n places, respectively.
3. $T = (t_1, t_2, \ldots, t_q)$ is a finite set of transitions.
4. $F \subseteq (P \times T) \bigcup (T \times P)$ is a finite set of arcs (associations).
5. $W : F \to (1, 2, \ldots)$ is a finite set of weights for these arcs.

An incidence matrix, C, can be derived from the associations, F, and the weight function, W. Element c_{pt} of this matrix is calculated using the weights of the two arcs (one input and one output) connecting place p to transition t:

$$C_{pt} = w(t, p) - w(p, t) \tag{1.1}$$

Petri nets have been shown to be useful in software design, data analysis, process modeling, and many other applications. The use of Petri nets has also been extended into information and computer security. The ability of Petri nets to capture concurrent interactions is especially useful for the analysis of security [15]. As an example, Chen *et al.* [16] propose the use of Petri nets to model attacks on cyber-physical systems. While the paper does not provide a complete model, it does describe methods to represent physical as well as cyber attacks. They also discuss a method to address the scalability of the model.

Classical Petri nets have limitations that reduce their modeling and decision power. Time is not represented in classical Petri nets—the model analysis is based upon immediate "firing" of a transition when its preconditions are met. Each transition is treated as an event, but some events may take longer than others. The lack of timing information in a classical Petri net model prevents it from representing the sojourn time in each state or the time required to reach a given state. Adding a time component to the model facilitates representation of delays or timed events. In timed Petri nets, timing can be associated with places, where the place holds a token for a given duration before enabling firing of the corresponding transition [17]. Alternatively, a firing duration can be associated with a transition [18] or an arc. These three options are compared in Ref. [19].

2.4 Stochastic Petri Nets

Another limitation of classic Petri nets is the inability to represent nondeterministic events–transitions (deterministically) fire when they are enabled. In order to add timing and probability to the model, we introduce stochastic Petri nets. Stochastic Petri nets give us the ability to bring both timing and randomness to the model. A common example for stochastic Petri nets is to model the use of a light bulb. We know that it can be on, off, or "burned out." During the lifetime of the bulb, turning it on or off is a deliberate action, with deterministic results. The lifetime is a random variable. Bulbs most commonly burn out immediately after being switched on, but it could "burn out" from an off state as well; for example, vibration could cause a fragile filament to break. A stochastic Petri net can enumerate the various states of the bulb, and the transitions among them, while representing the nondeterministic nature of the transitions between these states. Timed and stochastic Petri nets, which allow for nondeterministic firing times [20,21], are especially useful in modeling security, as they more realistically capture the nondeterministic approach and progression of a typical attack, which rarely progresses in a predictable fashion. For example, both brute force and phishing may be attempted in a password attack, and either attempt can lead to a compromised state for the system. The order in which the attempts are made and their likelihood of success is unpredictable, making a stochastic Petri net an appropriate choice for modeling the attack.

A disadvantage of the basic stochastic Petri net is the inability to handle instantaneous transitions. Generalized stochastic Petri nets were introduced to address this shortcoming and can represent both instantaneous and timed transitions [22]. To continue the example above, an instantaneous transition is one in which the attacker would use a known exploit to reach an unsafe state in the model—the attack could be considered instantaneously successful.

In a related application, stochastic Petri nets have been used to predict software security [23], by determining the probability of a successful attack based on the number of tokens in unsafe states. Other examples include the modeling of Trojan exploits [24] and power system security [25].

In closing, timed and stochastic Petri nets are powerful models capable of accurate representation of a broad range of vulnerabilities and exploits. This realism makes them appropriate for decision support related to system security. Section 3 elaborates upon and illustrates these abilities.

3. MODEL-BASED ANALYSIS OF SYSTEM SECURITY

This section illustrates model-based security analysis through the simple example of a memory chip—a fundamental building block of any information system. The first step in developing a security model is the enumeration of all potential breaches of security. In our example, the chip can be compromised in three fashions. The first would be unauthorized access to some or all of its data, corresponding to the first pillar of security—confidentiality. Unauthorized modification of data on the chip compromises the second pillar of security—integrity. Finally, preventing legitimate access to the data would violate the third pillar of security—availability. The next step in developing a security model relates to understanding the system—which components exhibit vulnerabilities that could lead to each compromise? Vulnerability, exposure, and/or risk assessments can be used to this end. Comprehensive representation of system security necessitates consideration of all of its aspects, which may overlap. Examples include human security, physical security, systems/communication protections, integrity, access control, and media protection.

We seek to compare the two modeling approaches described in Section 2—attack graphs and Petri nets, in terms of their accuracy and ability to facilitate decision support, respectively. The former has been investigated for Petri nets in Ref. [26]. We were unable to identify any studies that examine models based on the latter.

More specifically, we define accuracy as the ability of a model to describe the characteristics and states of a system. This is a qualitative metric for which we consider three levels:

1. Accuracy is *high* when a model can accurately describe a system and *all* of its potential states. In our example, the goal is to identify all possible states of a memory chip. Only a model capable of representing every possible state would be considered highly accurate.

2. Accuracy is *moderate* when a model can accurately describe a system and *most* of its potential states.
3. Accuracy is *low* when a model can provide a general description for a system and *some* of its potential states.

A noteworthy trade-off exists between the accuracy and complexity of a model. In cases of potential state-space explosion, a less accurate model may be the only computationally feasible option.

The second criterion we use in comparing security models is *decision power*—the ability to facilitate decision support by providing definitive security-related information about the system. This metric is also qualitative, and we similarly consider three levels of decision power:

1. Decision power is *high* when a model provides *definitive* security-related information about *all* potential states of a system.
2. Decision power is *moderate* when a model provides *some definitive and some general* security-related information about *most* potential states of a system.
3. Decision power is *low* when a model provides *general* security-related information about a system and *some* of its potential states.

In our example, the goal is to identify specific states or sequence of states that will lead to an exploit of a memory chip. If a model is able to capture all undesirable states and/or security information related to the system, it would be considered to have high decision power. If the model cannot provide an exhaustive description of the information security, then it would be rated at one of the lower levels. It should be noted that the decision power of a model is contingent upon its accuracy.

3.1 Security Analysis Based on Classical Attack Graph Model

Attack graphs can be created using quantitative and/or qualitative descriptive processes. The use of the common vulnerabilities and exploits database and network vulnerability scanning are two common quantitative processes. Qualitative descriptive processes normally include enumeration of environmental variables and likely attacks. One of the shortcomings of classical attack graphs is that they are static and do not take into account information from the environment or attempts toward defending the system. Incorporation of these attack trees has been enhanced by adding defensive information into the graph [27]. Despite the addition, the model remains static. The lack of timing information or consideration of nondeterminism is another impediment to the utility of these attack graphs.

Formal analysis of attack graphs is limited. The most common analysis method is determining reachability [28]. The graph is drawn, and all possible paths connecting the initial node to the goal node are enumerated. By adding attributes to each node, reachability analysis can be extended to consideration of cost, difficulty, or other measures associated with a path.

Model checking, a formal analysis technique used in systems engineering and related fields, is also used in the analysis of attack graphs [29]. Model checking ensures that the attack graph represents only feasible states. Adjacency matrix clustering [28], minimization analysis [30], ranking graphs [31], and game theory approaches [32] have also been used for the analysis of attack graphs.

Table 1.1 identifies several methods of attack graph analysis and compares them in terms of decision power and accuracy. Sections 3.1.1 through 3.1.4 illustrates a subset of these methods by application to the example depicted in Fig. 1.1.

3.1.1 Reachability Analysis

In the attack graph of Fig. 1.1, compromise of the system is possible through the four paths described in Table 1.2. The model allows a defender to understand and visualize the attack methods that can be used to exploit the system and, as such, offers high decision power. The accuracy is low due to the fact that the model in its original form does not provide information about system properties that could be relevant to the path taken to achieve the breach.

3.1.2 Minimization Analysis

Paths 1 and 4 are the shortest paths an attacker can use to reach the goal. In addition, the analysis shows that all attacks must go through node 2—a key point in the defense of the system. The decision power is due to the ability to identify the minimum number of exploits required. This decision power is moderate, rather than high, as the difficulty of path is not taken into consideration—the shortest path may also be the most difficult.

3.1.3 Model Checking Analysis

Model checking determines whether the system satisfies a given property. In attack graphs, that property is security—the goal is to determine whether any of the states or properties of a system make it insecure. Using the reachability paths, it can be shown that insecure states exist in the attack graph of Fig. 1.1. The advantage of model checking is the ability to identify insecure states using widely available tools. This is the source of the decision

Table 1.1 Analysis Methods for Attack Graphs

Analysis Method	Description	Decision Power	Accuracy
Reachability [28]	Enumerates all possible paths toward the goal. Accuracy and decision power depend on whether all exploits and goals are represented.	High	Moderate
Minimization	Determines the "shortest" route to the goal, or the exploit likely to be used in the greatest number of attacks. Does not provide fine-grained information about the system when used in isolation.	Moderate	Moderate
Model checking [29]	Verifies the feasibility of the states of a model.	Moderate	Moderate
Attribute [28]	Provides the ability to refine the model by adding attributes to nodes (or arcs). The static nature of attack graphs limits the utility of this technique, as it does not allow for consideration of addition or update of attributes, or their relationships.	High	Moderate
Adjacency matrix clustering [28]	Provides the ability to reduce the complexity of the model, while representing all potential states and identifying single- or multiuser attacks. Of limited use without the addition of attributes.	Moderate	High
Ranking graph [31]	Combines model checking with ranking algorithms that determine the importance of states in a model.	Low	High
Game theory [32]	Converts an attack graph into a two-player stochastic game, for which it constructs a model and computes the Nash equilibrium.	Moderate	Moderate

Table 1.2 Reachability Analysis for Fig. 1.1

Path	Description
Path 1	1,2,3,4
Path 2	1,2,5,6,4
Path 3	1,2,5,7,4
Path 4	1,2,8,4

power of the method. The accuracy of the model is limited by the need to prevent state-space explosion. Furthermore, attack graph models treat states as atomic, eliminating the possibility of extracting information about the state history.

3.1.4 Attribute Analysis

The attributes we add to Fig. 1.1 are node difficulty and node cost. The difficulty level ranges from 1 to 5, with 5 denoting the greatest difficulty. The cost, which increases if special tools or equipment are required to perform the task, ranges from 1 to 5, with 5 denoting the greatest cost. Table 1.3 shows the assignment of difficulty and cost to the nodes of Fig. 1.1. Table 1.4 calculates the difficulty and cost of each of the four possible attack paths. This ability to compare attacks in terms of their attributes is the source of the decision power of this model.

Addition of the difficulty and cost attributes increases the accuracy and decision power of the attack graph. Previously unavailable information can now be ascertained; for example, that path 4 is the most difficult attack because the attacker may need special tools or expertise. The cost of all the attacks is the same, with the exception of path 4. Observation of the attributes and paths leads to the conclusion that easiest and least expensive way to compromise a memory chip is to physically damage it. This information is useful to the defender in deciding on fortification

Table 1.3 Node Difficulty and Cost

Node	Difficulty	Cost
Node 1	2	2
Node 2	2	2
Node 3	2	2
Node 4	2	3
Node 5	3	1
Node 6	2	1
Node 7	3	1
Node 8	10	1

Table 1.4 Path Difficulty and Cost

Path	Path	Difficulty	Cost
1	1,2,3,4	8	9
2	1,2,5,6,4	11	9
3	1,2,5,7,4	12	9
4	1,2,8,4	16	8

techniques—in this case, ensuring physical or personnel security may be the best defense.

3.2 Security Analysis Based on the Stochastic Attack Graph Model

Stochastic attack graphs capture the nondeterminism inherent to any potential security compromise. The resulting security analysis can be carried out through methods similar to those mentioned in Section 3.1 for classical attack graphs. Among these methods, we focus on the two methods that leverage the probabilistic nature of stochastic attack graphs: state risk–level and stochastic shortest path analysis, respectively. Table 1.5 describes both models.

3.2.1 State Risk-Level Analysis

The objective of this method is to determine the probability that an attacker will reach a specific state within a stochastic attack graph. As such, state risk-level analysis can be considered as an enhancement of the reachability analysis described for classical attack graphs. The ability to consider nondeterministic reachability increases both accuracy and decision power of stochastic attack graphs over their classical counterparts.

3.2.2 Stochastic Shortest Path Analysis

This method can be considered an enhancement to the minimization analysis described for classical attack graphs, as it considers the probability of success of each path and assumes that paths more likely to succeed are more likely to be taken by the attacker. The stochastic shortest path problem aims to determine for a stochastic graph the path guaranteed to reach a given target state with minimum expected cost. An MDP, which associates a "cost" or "reward" value with each transition, is used to this end [33]. In the memory chip example, the stochastic shortest path is not the same as its deterministic counterpart, due to the fact that the probability of damaging a

Table 1.5 Analysis Methods for Stochastic Attack Graphs

Analysis Method	Description	Decision Power	Accuracy
State risk level	Determines the probability of reaching a target state	High	Moderate
Stochastic shortest path	Determines the path guaranteed to reach a given target state with minimum expected cost	Moderate	Moderate

memory chip is higher than that of reading the data from the chip before it is powered on. The consideration of nondeterminism increases both accuracy and decision power of the model. In security analysis using classical attack graphs, the best we could do was to add attributes from which probabilities can be inferred. These attributes are in many cases qualitative rather than quantitative, reducing the accuracy and decision power of the classical attack graph model.

4. SECURITY ANALYSIS BASED ON PETRI NETS

As any other security model, we aimed at utilizing a Petri net that will have high accuracy and decision power, both of which are constrained by consequences of model complexity. In this section, we begin by developing a Petri net-based security model for the memory chip exploit and discuss the accuracy and decision power of this model, which can be considered the dynamic counterpart of the attack graph of Fig. 1.1. We subsequently extend this model to a stochastic Petri net and discuss its accuracy and decision power.

Using the notation presented in Section 2.3, the Petri net of Fig. 1.3 can be described as follows:

1. $P = (p_1, p_2, \ldots, p_5)$ is the set of places.
2. $m_0 = (1, 0, 0, 0, 0)$ is the initial marking.
3. $T = (t_1, t_2, \ldots, t_8)$ is the set of transitions.
4. The weight of every existing arc (connecting a place to a transition) is one unit.
5. Element C_{pt} of the incidence matrix is determined as $w(t, p) - w(p, t)$.

$$
C = \begin{bmatrix}
-1 & 0 & 0 & 0 & 0 & 0 & 0 & 0 \\
1 & -1 & -1 & -1 & 0 & 0 & 0 & 0 \\
0 & 0 & 1 & 0 & -1 & -1 & -1 & 0 \\
0 & 0 & 0 & 1 & 0 & 0 & 0 & -1 \\
0 & 1 & 0 & 0 & 1 & 1 & 1 & 1
\end{bmatrix}
$$

4.1 Security Analysis Based on Classical Petri Nets

A Petri net model can be analyzed behaviorally or structurally. Both types of analysis provide useful information about the model. *Behavioral analysis* focuses on the various states that result for a Petri net during the movement of tokens and firing of transitions. *Structural analysis* focuses on the properties

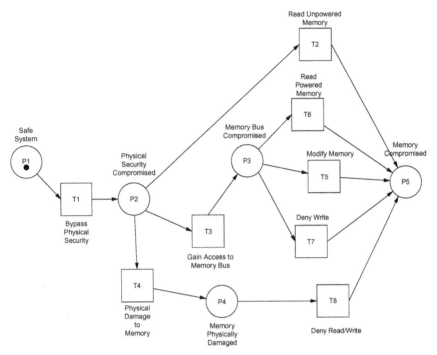

Figure 1.3 Classical Petri net of memory exploit—physical security.

of the Petri net, based on the incidence matrix and independent of the initial marking. The dynamic nature of behavioral analysis makes it more useful in security analysis, and as such, our focus for the remainder of this section will be on behavioral analysis.

4.1.1 Behavioral Analysis of Petri Nets

Behavioral analysis considers (i) the initial marking of the Petri net and (ii) its reachability graph. The reachability graph of a Petri net is a directed graph, $G = (V, E)$, where each node, $v \in V$, represents a reachable marking and each edge, $e \in E$, represents a transition between two reachable markings. The set of reachable markings can be infinite, even for a finite Petri net. In such cases, a coverability tree is constructed instead. The reachability graph for our example Petri net of Fig. 1.3 is depicted in Fig. 1.4.

Once the reachability graph is constructed, a number of behavioral properties can be evaluated [34]. We discuss four main properties in the context of the memory chip exploit example. These and additional behavioral properties are summarized in Table 1.6.

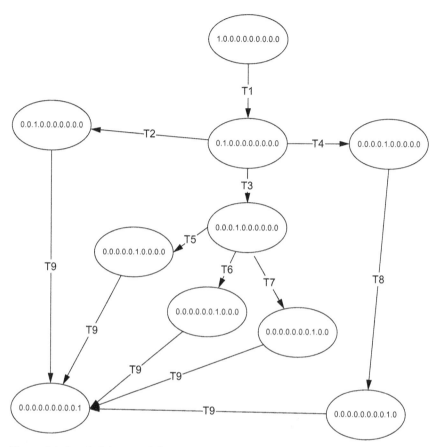

Figure 1.4 Reachability graph for the Petri net of Fig. 1.3.

Reachability This is evaluated for each state of the Petri net, identifying states that could be reached in a feasible compromise. From Fig. 1.4, it is evident that multiple paths can lead to compromise of the memory chip. The results of reachability analysis for the Petri net of a system should be consistent with the findings of reachability analysis of its attack graph.

Shortest path This analysis utilizes the reachability graph to determine the shortest path to compromise. In our example, the shortest path is between (1.0.0.0.0) and (0.1.0.0.0).

Boundedness and safeness Each place in a Petri net is evaluated (using the reachability graph) to determine whether it contains at most k tokens in each reachable marking, including the initial marking. If

Table 1.6 Behavioral Analysis Metrics

Property	Description	Decision Power	Accuracy
Reachability	Determines whether a given marking can be reached from the initial marking through a sequential set of transitions.	High	High
Coverability	Determines whether a specific marking of the Petri net can be reached. This property is used instead of reachability in cases where we need to determine whether the system can be compromised in a specific way.	High	High
Boundedness	This property is useful in analyzing multiple concurrent attacks. Places that accumulate tokens can be identified and flagged as critical. The Petri net model of a single attack is safe and bounded, as one token exists in the net at any point in time.	High	High
Liveness	Identifies transitions that will never be able to fire, indicating that the corresponding exploit is infeasible. Conversely, a live transition can always fire, and as such is a significant vulnerability.	High	High
Reversibility	Since the goal is to compromise the system, determining reversibility would only confirm the information gained from reachability and coverability. Useful for identification of security breaches that are likely to go undetected.	Low	Low
Repetitivity	Repetition of a successful attack does not supply additional information to the defender, and as such, this property is of limited use in security analysis.	Low	Low
Persistence	Determines whether a marking exists where a transition is disabled due to the firing of another transition. This information would be beneficial in determining ways to prevent or stop an attack.	High	Low
Consistency	Identifies transitions that are not possible. This could aid in decisions regarding defensive measures.	High	Medium
Conservation	Indicative of a net that creates more tokens than are consumed. Beneficial for analysis of multiple concurrent attacks.	High	Low

Table 1.6 Behavioral Analysis Metrics—cont'd

Property	Description	Decision Power	Accuracy
Synchronic distance	Determines the steps needed to reach a compromise state from any state. In security, this could be associated with difficulty or cost to compromise. The higher the number of steps, the greater the difficult or cost of the attack.	High	High
Fairness	Indicates that the selection from among enabled transitions is fair. The lack of fairness could facilitate the identification of transitions that fire disproportionately often. Additional defensive measures are necessary for these exploits.	High	High

this is the case, the place is considered k-bounded. If $k = 1$, the place is considered *safe*. If every place in a Petri net is k-bounded, the net as a whole is considered to be *bounded*. If every place is safe, the Petri net is considered safe. If we extend our example to consider software attacks such as attempts to cause buffer overflow, the boundedness and safety characteristics would help in identifying places where the accumulation of tokens could cause buffer overflow.

Liveness A transition is considered *dead* if it can never fire. It is considered live if it can fire in every reachable marking. Liveness implies that no deadlock exists in the system represented by the Petri net. In the security context, liveness implies that nothing prevents an attacker from transitioning from any state to any other state.

Reversibility In the strict interpretation, a net is considered reversible if the initial marking m_0 can be reached from any marking in M. In the security context, reversibility implies that a compromised system could be returned to its initial state. This could eliminate the possibility of detecting the breach.

Persistence This indicates that once a transition is enabled, it will remain enabled. In other words, the precondition will remain true, and once the corresponding transition is fired, no conflict will occur among the resulting postcondition(s) [35]. Persistence in a net indicates the ability to perform actions in parallel. In the security context, this could occur as a result of simultaneous attempts at breaching the system.

4.2 Security Analysis Based on Stochastic Petri Nets

To create a stochastic Petri net, we extend the classical Petri net tuple $PN = (P, T, F, W, M)$, with an additional element, Λ, which is an array of firing rates associated with the transitions. We can then calculate the probability that a given transition will fire and change the marking, per:

$$P\{t_k|M_j\} = \frac{\lambda_k(M_j)}{\sum_{i:t_i \in E(M_j)} \lambda_i(M_j)}, \quad t_k \in E(M_j) \qquad (1.2)$$

Stochastic Petri nets are capable of capturing nondeterminism in various aspects of the model and typically incorporate time. In extending the Petri net of Fig. 1.3, we apply Eq. (1.2) to determine the probability that an enabled transition will fire. Similar to continuous-time Markov chains (CTMCs) and other Markovian models, stochastic Petri nets assume that the future state or marking of the model is independent of the marking history. This is important in information systems security, as it allows us to make decisions based upon the current state of the system instead of requiring the history of actions or states that led to the current state. An additional benefit is that we are able to leverage a large and mature body of tools and techniques developed for CTMCs.

Another advantage that the memoryless property provides to the model is the ability to enable or disable a given transition without resetting the time on other transitions. In other words, the model associates activities with transitions. When an activity completes, the state of the model changes, as denoted by a new marking, but other activities or transitions are not restarted due to the new marking. An attacker may attempt multiple attack vectors (OR function); the memoryless property implies that success in one transition would not automatically reset the attempt or timing of other vectors; for example, the transition to gain physical access does not automatically reset the counter for brute-force password attack.

The analysis techniques enumerated for classical Petri nets apply to their stochastic counterparts as well and attain similar accuracy and decision power. Consideration of nondeterminism will help to validate the reachability analysis—in any reachable marking, all enabled transitions should have a nonzero probability of firing. The reachability or coverability graph is constructed in the same manner as the classic Petri net, with the addition of the firing rates.

In the analysis of a stochastic Petri net, we seek to evaluate the following metrics, which are summarized in Table 1.7:

Table 1.7 Metrics Evaluated Through Stochastic Behavioral Analysis

Metric	Description	Decision Power	Accuracy
Probability of an event	$P\{A\} = \sum_{i:M \in E(M)} \pi_i$	High	High
pmf of tokens in a place	$p_i = P\{X = p_i\}$	Moderate	Moderate
Average number of tokens in a place	$E(X)$	Low	Moderate
Frequency of firing of a transition	$f_i = \sum_{i:t_j M \in E(M_i)} \lambda_j(M_i)\pi_i$	High	High
Average delay of a token	$E[T] = S\dfrac{E[N]}{E[\gamma]}$	High	High

Probability of a given event is a very valuable metric in terms of security analysis.

The probability mass function (pmf) of tokens in a place enhances the classical metric of boundedness by considering the probability that tokens are present or accumulating. This could point to critical states of strengths or weaknesses in the model.

The average number of tokens in a place serves as a summary of the pmf and is not as powerful as other metrics.

The firing frequency of a transition is very useful in security analysis, as it facilitates the identification of critical transitions in a model. If a given transition occurs frequently, defense of the system necessitates, ensuring that this transition leads to a secure state.

The average delay of a token in traversing the net provides information on the time needed to move the system from a secure state to an insecure state. This information could be used to determine tripwire placement.

5. CONCLUSIONS

The discussion in Section 3 elaborated on our original assertion—that dynamic models such as Petri nets are more powerful than their static counterparts, in particular attack graphs. Petri nets are more accurate and provide significantly greater decision support. Behavioral analysis of a Petri net can evaluate up to 14 properties, whereas attack graphs are limited to 4.

In terms of accuracy, Petri nets are—as expected—able to provide a representation with higher fidelity to the actual system, especially when extended to consider nondeterminism. The accuracy of attack graphs can be improved by adding attributes; however, analysis based on them remains static and has limited utility. Both models are prone to state-space explosion when applied to complex systems—Petri nets, as the more detailed model, are more vulnerable to this problem. Reducing the level of detail in the interest of computational feasibility also reduces the power of the model.

Consideration of nondeterminism extends the classical models to their stochastic counterparts. From stochastic attack graphs, we can evaluate two additional metrics: the state risk level and the stochastic shortest path. Stochastic Petri nets provide a greater enhancement to their classical base model. The conclusion remains the same: that stochastic Petri nets are more accurate and have greater decision power than stochastic attack graphs.

REFERENCES

[1] L. Piètre-Cambacédès, M. Bouissou, Beyond attack trees: dynamic security modeling with Boolean logic driven Markov processes (BDMP), in: Proceedings of the European Dependable Computing Conference (EDCC), 2010, pp. 199–208.
[2] J. Weiss, A system security engineering process, in: Proceedings of the 10th Annual Computer Security Applications Conference, 2004, pp. 80–83.
[3] K.S. Edge, A framework for analyzing and mitigating the vulnerabilities of complex systems via attack and protection trees, Ph.D. thesis, Air Force Institute of Technology, Wright Patterson Air Force Base, Ohio, 2007.
[4] S. Bistarelli, F. Fioravanti, P. Peretti, Defense trees for economic evaluation of security investments, in: Proceedings of 1st International Conference on Availability, Reliability and Security (ARES), 2006, pp. 416–423.
[5] M. McQueen, W. Boyer, M. Flynn, G. Beitel, Quantitative cyber risk reduction estimation methodology for a small SCADA control system, in: Proceedings of the 39th Annual Hawaii International Conference on System Sciences (HICSS), vol. 9, 2006, p. 226.
[6] S.C. Seo, J.H. You, Y.D. Kim, J.Y. Choi, S.J. Lee, B.K. Kim, Building security requirements using state transition diagram at security threat location, in: Proceedings of the International Conference on Computational Intelligence and Security (CIS), vol. II, Springer-Verlag, Berlin, Heidelberg, 2005, pp. 451–456.
[7] L. Piètree-Cambacédès, Y. Deflesselle, M. Bouissou, Security modeling with BDMP: from theory to implementation, in: Proceedings of the 6th IEEE International Conference on Network and Information System Security (SAR-SSI), La Rochelle, France, 2011, pp. 1–8.
[8] B. Schneier, Attack trees: modeling security threats, Dr. Dobbs J. 24 (12) (1999) 21–29.
[9] O. Sheyner, S. Jha, S. Haines, R. Lippmann, J.M. Wing, Automated generation and analysis of attack graphs, in: Proceedings of the IEEE Symposium on Security and Privacy, 2002, pp. 273–284.
[10] S. Noel, S. Jajodia, L. Wang, A. Singhal, Measuring security risk of networks using attack graphs, Int. J. Next-Generation Comput. 1 (1) (2010) 113–123.

[11] Y. Zhang, X. Fan, Z. Xue, H. Xu, Two stochastic models for security evaluation based on attack graph, in: Proceedings of the 9th International Conference for Young Computer Scientists (ICYCS), 2008, pp. 2198–2203.

[12] G. Dalton, R. Mills, J. Colombi, R. Raines, Analyzing attack trees using generalized stochastic Petri nets, in: Proceedings of the IEEE Information Assurance Workshop, 2006, pp. 116–123. http://dx.doi.org/10.1109/IAW.2006.1652085.

[13] J. Peterson, Petri Net Theory and the Modeling of Systems, Foundations of Philosophy, Prentice Hall PTR Upper Saddle River, NJ, USA, 1981.

[14] A. Halder, A study of Petri nets modeling, analysis, and simulation, Technical report, Indian Institute of Technology Kharagpur, Kharagpur, India, August 2006.

[15] J.-L. Yan, M.-X. He, T.-Y. Li, A Petri-net model of network security testing, in: Proceedings of the IEEE International Conference on Computer Science and Automation Engineering, 2011, pp. 188–192.

[16] T.M. Chen, S. Member, J.C. Sanchez-Aarnoutse, J. Buford, Petri net modeling of cyber-physical attacks on smart grid, IEEE Trans. Smart Grid 2 (4) (2011) 741–749.

[17] J. Sifakis, Use of Petri nets for performance evaluation, Acta Cybernet. 4 (2) (1979) 185–202.

[18] C. Ramchandani, Analysis of asynchronous concurrent systems by timed Petri nets, Technical report, Massachusetts Institute of Technology, Cambridge, MA, 1974.

[19] M. Boyer, O. Roux, Comparison of the expressiveness of arc, place and transition time Petri nets, in: J. Kleijn, A. Yakovlev (Eds.), Petri Nets and Other Models of Concurrency, Lecture Notes in Computer Science, vol. 4546, Springer, Berlin, Heidelberg, 2007, pp. 63–82.

[20] D. Kartson, G. Balbo, S. Donatelli, G. Franceschinis, G. Conte, Modelling with Generalized Stochastic Petri Nets, first ed., John Wiley & Sons, Inc., New York, NY, 1994.

[21] G. Balbo, Introduction to generalized stochastic Petri nets, in: M. Bernardo, J. Hillston (Eds.), Formal Methods for Performance Evaluation, Lecture Notes in Computer Science, vol. 4486, Springer, Berlin, Heidelberg, 2007, pp. 83–131.

[22] M. Ajmone Marsan, G. Conte, G. Balbo, A class of generalized stochastic Petri nets for the performance evaluation of multiprocessor systems, ACM Trans. Comput. Syst. 2 (2)(1984) 93–122.

[23] N. Yang, H. Yu, Z. Qian, H. Sun, Modeling and quantitatively predicting software security based on stochastic Petri nets, Math. Comput. Model. 55 (1–2) (2012) 102–112.

[24] H. Gao, Y. Wang, L. Wang, L. Liu, J. Li, X. Cheng, Trojan characteristics analysis based on stochastic Petri nets, in: Proceedings of the IEEE International Conference on Intelligence and Security Informatics (ISI), 2011, pp. 213–215.

[25] G. Ramos, J. Sanchez, A. Torres, M. Rios, Power systems security evaluation using Petri nets, IEEE Trans. Power Deliver. 25 (1) (2010) 316–322.

[26] G. Ciardo, Toward a definition of modeling power for stochastic Petri net models, in: Proceedings International Workshop on Petri Nets and Performance Models, 1987, pp. 54–62.

[27] T. Sommestad, M. Ekstedt, P. Johnson, Cyber security risks assessment with bayesian defense graphs and architectural models, in: Proceedings of the 42nd Hawaii International Conference on System Sciences (HICSS), 2009, pp. 1–10.

[28] S. Noel, S. Jajodia, Understanding complex network attack graphs through clustered adjacency matrices, in: Proceedings of the 21st Annual Computer Security Applications Conference (ACSAC), 2005, pp. 160–169.

[29] R. Ritchey, P. Ammann, Using model checking to analyze network vulnerabilities, in: Proceedings of the IEEE Symposium on Security and Privacy, 2000, pp. 156–165.

[30] S. Jha, O. Sheyner, J. Wing, Two formal analyses of attack graphs, in: Proceedings of the 15th IEEE Computer Security Foundations Workshop, 2002, pp. 49–63.
[31] V. Mehta, C. Bartzis, H. Zhu, E. Clarke, J. Wing, Ranking attack graphs, in: D. Zamboni, C. Kruegel (Eds.), Recent Advances in Intrusion Detection, Lecture Notes in Computer Science, vol. 4219, Springer, Berlin, Heidelberg, 2006, pp. 127–144.
[32] K.-W. Lye, J.M. Wing, Game strategies in network security, Int. J. Inform. Security 4 (1–2) (2005) 71–86.
[33] D.P. Bertsekas, J.N. Tsitsiklis, An analysis of stochastic shortest path problems, Math. Oper. Res. 16 (1991) 580–595.
[34] X. Ye, J. Zhou, X. Song, On reachability graphs of Petri nets, Comput. Electr. Eng. 29 (2) (2003) 263–272.
[35] F. Crazzolara, G. Winskel, Petri nets with persistence, Electron. Notes Theor. Comput. Sci. 121 (2005) 143–155.

ABOUT THE AUTHORS

Steven C. White, PhD student, received his BS in Electrical Engineering in 1992 and MS in Information Science & Technology in 2006 at the Missouri University of Science and Technology. Steve is currently working toward a PhD in Computer Engineering. Steve's interests involve information security and security modeling. Of particular interest is security in the enterprise environment. This involves developing security models for complex cyber systems and information systems. Currently, Steve works as an assistant director in the Information and Communication Technology Division of the Missouri State Highway Patrol.

Dr. Sahra Sedigh Sarvestani is an associate professor of Electrical and Computer Engineering and a research investigator with the Intelligent Systems Center at the Missouri University of Science and Technology. Her current research centers on development and modeling of dependable networks and systems, with focus on critical infrastructure. She received the BS degree from the Sharif University of Technology and the MS and PhD degrees from Purdue University, all in electrical engineering. She is a fellow of the National Academy of Engineering's First Frontiers of Engineering Education Symposium. She held a Purdue Research Foundation Fellowship from 1996 to 2000 and is a member of HKN, IEEE, and ACM.

CHAPTER TWO

A Survey on Zero-Knowledge Proofs

Li Feng, Bruce McMillin

Deparment of Computer Science, Missouri University of Science and Technology, Rolla, Missouri, USA

Contents

Advances in Computers, Volume 94
ISSN 0065-2458
http://dx.doi.org/10.1016/B978-0-12-800161-5.00002-5

25

Abstract

Zero-knowledge proofs (ZKPs) are interactive protocols in which one party, named the prover, can convince the other party, named the verifier, that some assertion is true without revealing anything other than the fact that the assertion being proven is true. This chapter is a survey on ZKPs including their background, important concepts, applications for NP problems, and composition operations of ZKPs. The remarkable property of being both convincing and yielding nothing except that the assertion is indeed valid makes ZKPs very powerful tools for the design of secure cryptographic protocols. In this chapter, ZKPs are constructed for the exact cover and 0–1 simple knapsack problem.

1. BACKGROUND AND MOTIVATION

In order to deal with the problem of distrustful parties convincing each other that the message they are sending is indeed computed according to their predetermined procedure without yielding any secret knowledge, a number of privacy-preserving communication protocols have been proposed and designed, including, for example, the fuzzy vault scheme, k-anonymity, nondeducibility, zero-knowledge proofs (ZKPs), and so on.

Shamir provided a scheme to share a secret in Ref. [1]. Rather than straightforward encryption, the main idea is to divide data D into n pieces in such a way that D is easily reconstructible from any k pieces, but even combining $k - 1$ pieces will not reveal any information about D. This scheme is called a (k, n) threshold scheme. Threshold schemes are ideally suited to applications in which a group of mutually suspicious individuals with conflicting interests must cooperate.

The fuzzy vault is a novel cryptographic notion developed by Juels and Sudan [2], which can be considered as a form of error-tolerant encryption operation. In a fuzzy vault scheme, one party places a secret value k in a fuzzy vault and "locks" it using a set A of elements from some public universe U; the other party can "unlock" the vault to get the secret value k using a set B of similar length only if A and B overlap substantially. A fuzzy fault scheme can be constructed based on any type of linear error–correcting code.

Another privacy-preserving framework for communication is called k-anonymity. A data record is k-anonymous if and only if it is indistinguishable in its identifying information from at least k specific records. k-Anonymity provides a formal way of preventing reidentification of data to fewer than a group of k data items. k-Anonymity provides a formal way of generalizing aggregated data without violating the privacy [3].

Nondeducibility is a security model based on information theory, especially for information sharing. The model states that information flows in a system from high-level objects to low-level objects if and only if some possible assignment of values to the low-level objects in the state is incompatible with a possible assignment of values to the state's high-level objects [4]. To be more specific, a system is considered nondeducible secure if it is impossible for a low-level user, through observing visible events, to deduce anything about the sequence of inputs made by a high-level user.

The notion of ZKPs, which is first introduced by Goldwasser *et al.* [5], is to obtain a system in which it is possible for a prover to convince a verifier of his knowledge of an assertion without disclosing any information except the validity of his assertion. ZKP study has become a very active research area because of its fascinating nature of a seemingly contradictory definition; ZKPs have the remarkable property of being both convincing and yielding nothing except that the assertion is indeed valid, which makes them very powerful tools for the design of a secure cryptographic protocol [6].

2. INTRODUCTION

2.1 Interactive Proof and Its Properties

Before presenting the definition of ZKPs, we first introduce the notion of an overarching class, the interactive proof.

Definition 2.1 (Interactive Proof [5]) *An interactive proof system for a language L is a pair of interactive Turing machines, (P, V) in which V, the verifier, executing a probabilistic polynomial-time strategy and P, the prover, executing a computationally unbounded strategy, satisfy two properties: completeness and soundness.*

- Completeness can be expressed as

$$Prob[(P, V)(x) = 1 \mid x \in L] \geq 1 - |x|^{-c} \ (c > 0)$$

- Soundness can be expressed for every interactive Turing machine P^* as

$$Prob[(P^*, V)(x) = 0 \mid x \notin L] \geq 1 - |x|^{-c} \ (c > 0)$$

Completeness means that the verifier accepts the proof if the statement or assertion is true. In another words, an honest verifier will always be convinced of a true statement by an honest prover. Soundness means that if the fact is false, the verifier rejects the proof, which indicates that a cheating prover can convince an honest verifier that some false statement is actually true with only a small probability. Both conditions allow a negligible error probability, which plays an important role in ZKPs with a robust notion of rareness; a rare event should occur rarely even if we repeat the experiment for a feasible number of times [7].

Proofs here do not represent the traditional mathematical concept of a proof. Mathematical proofs are strict, either using self-evident statements obtained or from proofs established beforehand. Here, proofs are not a fixed and static object; they are similar to the dynamic process used to establish the truth of a statement throughout the exchange of information. Thus, they are considered to be probabilistic rather than absolute. The class of problems having interactive proof systems is denoted as IP [7].

2.2 A Simple Example

"In cryptography, the ZKP is an interactive method for one party to prove to another that a statement is true, without revealing anything other than the veracity of the statement [6]." Each party in the protocol does a sequence of actions. While receiving a message from the other party, it performs a private computation and then it sends a message to the other party. Those actions will be repeated many rounds. Then, the verifier either accepts or rejects the prover's proof.

A very simple example of a ZKP could be illustrated as a story of Ali Baba's Cave [8]. In this story, Fig. 2.1, Peggy (the prover) has uncovered the secret word used to open a magic door in a cave. The cave is shaped like a circle, with the entrance on one side and the magic door blocking the opposite side. Victor (the verifier) says he will pay her for the secret, but not until he is sure that she really knows it. Peggy says she will tell him the secret, but not until she receives the money. They devise a scheme by which Peggy can prove that she knows the word without telling it to Victor. Peggy goes into a random branch of the cave without letting Victor knowing which branch she chose. Standing at the entrance to the cave, Victor calls out a

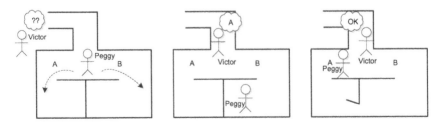

Figure 2.1 Ali Baba's Cave.

random branch he wants Peggy to come out from. If Peggy indeed knows about the secret password, she can obey every time. If she does not know the secret password, she has a 50% of initially fooling Victor. If Victor is happy with a 1 in 1024 chance that Peggy is cheating, there will be 10 iterations since $1/2^{10} = 1/1024$.

2.3 Computational Indistinguishability

"Effective similarity" is a widely accepted notion in Modern Cryptography. If the differences between the objects cannot be observed through a feasible computation, then the two objects are considered equivalent. In the definition of zero knowledge, it is impossible to tell the differences among computationally indistinguishable objects. The notion of computational indistinguishability underlies the definition of general zero knowledge [7].

For $S \subseteq \{0, 1\}^*$, the probability ensembles $X = \{X_\alpha\}_{\alpha \in S}$ and $Y = \{Y_\alpha\}_{\alpha \in S}$ contain X_α and Y_α, which is a distribution that ranges over strings of length polynomial in $|\alpha|$. A polynomial-size circuit $\{D_n\}$ means that there exists a deterministic Turing machine which has a running time polynomial in n on the circuit. $\Pr[D_n(X_\alpha) = 1]$ denotes the probability that circuit D_n outputs 1 on input X_α.

Definition 2.2 (Computational Indistinguishability [9,10]) $X = \{X_\alpha\}_{\alpha \in S}$ and $Y = \{Y_\alpha\}_{\alpha \in S}$ are computationally indistinguishable if for every family of polynomial-size circuits $\{D_n\}$, every polynomial p, and sufficiently large n and every $\alpha \in \{0, 1\}^n \cap S$,

$$|\Pr[D_n(X_\alpha) = 1] - \Pr[D_n(Y_\alpha) = 1]| < \frac{1}{p(n)}$$

where the probabilities are taken over the relevant distribution.

2.4 One-Way Function

In general, Modern Cryptography is always concerned with a question of whether one-way functions exist. One-way functions provide us the equivalent of digital lockable boxes. They are functions that are easy to evaluate but hard (on the average) to invert, which has an intractability characteristic.

Definition 2.3 (One–Way Function [7]) A function $f : \{0, 1\}^* \rightarrow \{0, 1\}^*$ is called one way if the following two conditions hold:
1. Easy to evaluate: There exists a polynomial-time algorithm A such that $A(x) = f(x)$ for every $x \in \{0, 1\}^*$.

2. *Hard to invert: For every family of polynomial-size circuits* $\{C_n\}$, *every polynomial p, and all sufficiently large n,*

$$\Pr[C_n(f(x)) \in f^{-1}(f(x))] < \frac{1}{p(n)}$$

where the probability is taken uniformly over all the possible choices of $x \in \{0,\ 1\}^n$.

Because the problem of factoring large integers is computationally intractable, the function that takes as input two (equal length) primes and outputs their product is widely believed to be a one-way function [3].

2.5 Simulation Paradigm

The simulation paradigm is another important notion, which was first developed in the context of zero knowledge, presented by Goldwasser, Micali, and Rackoff [5]. The crucial point is that for every algorithm that represents the strategy of the verifier, there exists a simulator that can simulate the entire interaction of the verifier and the honest prover without access to the prover's auxiliary information. It is an approach which makes the adversary gains nothing if whatever it can obtain by unrestricted adversarial behavior can be obtained within essentially the same computational effort as the prover. In this way, the adversary gains nothing.

A simulator is defined as a method or a procedure that generates fake (generated without the prover) views that are indistinguishable from a genuine (generated with the prover) view of a proof [12]. To be more specific, whatever a verifier might have learned from the interaction with the prover, he could have actually learned by himself by running the simulator. Figure 2.2 illustrates the idea. The concept of a simulator helps defining the zero-knowledge property in another way; that is, a proof of knowledge has the zero-knowledge property if there exists a simulator for the proof.

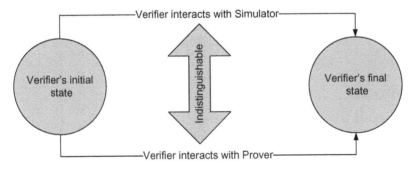

Figure 2.2 Simulator.

2.6 Definition of ZKP

Based on the above important concepts, ZKP is defined as an interactive proof system with zero knowledge. The zero-knowledge property means that no amount of knowledge should pass between the prover and the verifier.

Definition 2.4 (Zero Knowledge [5]) *An interactive strategy A is auxiliary-input zero knowledge on inputs from the set S if, for every probabilistic polynomial-time (interactive) strategy B^* and every polynomial p, there exists a probabilistic polynomial-time (noninteractive) algorithm C^* such that the following two probability ensembles are computationally indistinguishable [7]:*

1. *$\{(A, B^*(z))(x)\}_{x \in S,\ z \in \{0,\ 1\}^{p(|x|)}} \overset{\text{def}}{=}$ the output of B^* when having auxiliary-input z and interacting with A on common input $x \in S$; and*

2. *$\{C^*(x, z)\}_{x \in S,\ z \in \{0,1\}^{p(|x|)}} \overset{\text{def}}{=}$ the output of C^* on input $x \in S$, $z \in \{0, 1\}^{p(|x|)}$.*

The first one represents an actual execution of an interactive protocol. The second one represents the computation of a stand-alone procedure: the simulator does not interact with anybody. The more basic definition of zero knowledge is obtained by eliminating the auxiliary input z from this definition. But, almost all known ZKPs are in fact auxiliary-input zero knowledge.

Since whatever can be extracted from interaction with A on input $x \in S$ can also be extracted from x itself, nothing was gained by the interaction itself. Thus, in the concept of ZKPs, the verifier does not obtain further information about the assertion other than its validity. Furthermore, there is no degradation with repeated usage of ZKPs, which means that the number of iterations the protocol runs will not change the chances of success of obtaining the secret.

Zero knowledge is a security property which could protect the prover from leaking unnecessary information to any verifier.

2.7 Witness Indistinguishability

The notion of witness indistinguishability (WI) was introduced by Feige and Shamir in Ref. [13], which means the view of any verifier is "computationally independent" of the witness that is used by the honest prover as auxiliary private input.

NP, that refers to "nondeterministic polynomial time", is the set of all decision problems for which the answer "yes" can be verified in polynomial time. Loosely speaking, for any NP relation, an argument system for the corresponding language is called WI if no feasible verifier can distinguish the case in which the prover uses one NP witness to some input from the case in which the prover is using a different NP witness to the same input [7].

A witness is defined as a string w such that $(x, w) \in R$ [11]. For a binary relation R, $L(R)$ is defined as

$$\{x | \exists \ w \ s.t \ (x, w) \in R\}$$

Specifically, when proving that a string x is in $L(R)$, the prover gets a witness w such that $(x, w) \in R$. If the proof system is WI, then for any w, w' such that $(x, w) \in R, (x, w') \in R$, and for any polynomial-size verifier, the view of the verifier when interacting with the prover that uses w as auxiliary input is computationally indistinguishable from its view when interacting with the prover that uses w' as auxiliary input. The WI property is preserved under arbitrary composition of protocols [13].

2.8 Honest Verifier Versus General Cheating Verifier

The definition of zero knowledge refers to all feasible verifiers as either honest or cheating. Typically, the verifier is viewed as an adversary that is trying to cheat and attempt to gain something by interacting with the prover. With respect to the honest verifier, it will interact with the prover as expected, excepting that it may also maintain a record of the entire interaction and output this record in the end [7].

2.9 Black-Box Simulator Versus Non-Black-Box Simulator

The definition of zero knowledge requires that the interaction of the prover with any verifier is computationally indistinguishable with an ordinary probabilistic polynomial-time machine that interacts with no one.

Since whatever can be computed after interacting with a prover can be computed on any random input by itself, the ZKP is computationally equivalent to a trusted oracle. This is the notion of a black-box simulator. A black-box simulator is one that can simulate the interaction of the prover with any such a verifier when given oracle access to the strategy of that verifier. To be more specific, a black-box simulator indicates that using any verifier as a black box produces fake views that are indistinguishable from the verifier's actual interaction with the prover [11]. Most of the previous ZKPs or arguments are established using a black-box simulator.

But how can the simulator generate an interaction that is indistinguishable from the actual interaction with the prover? First, the simulator has access to the verifier's random question transcript, which means it can actually determine the next question that the verifier is going to ask. Second, the simulator has many ways to answer the verifier's questions. The technique is called rewinding which means if the simulator fails to answer a question provided by the verifier, it simply rewinds the verifier back and asks again [11].

However, when using the verifier's strategy as a black box, it is hard for the simulator to take advantage of the knowledge of the verifier's random question transcript. Therefore, there are restrictions and negative results while applying black-box simulator. Goldreich and Krawczyk [14] have shown nonexistence of black-box three-round ZKPs where a round defines number of steps in the protocol.

In order to overcome the restrictions of black-box simulators, non-black-box simulators were developed. The power of non-black-box simulators has been discovered by Barak [11]. Barak has shown how to construct non-black-box simulators and obtained several results which are considered to be unachievable through a black-box simulator. He presented a zero-knowledge argument system for NP with the following properties:

- It is the first zero-knowledge argument with a constant number of rounds and negligible soundness error.
- It is an Arthur–Merlin (public coins) protocol. The Arthur–Merlin protocol, introduced by Babai [15], is an interactive proof system in which the verifier's coin tosses are known to the prover too.
- It has a strict polynomial-time simulator rather than expected polynomial time.

By taking advantage of the strategies of the verifier, since the knowledge of the verifier is not an oracle in non-black-box simulator, Barak's result calls for the reevaluation of many common beliefs, such as nonexistence of (black-box) three-round ZKPs and impossibility of (black-box) constant-round concurrent zero knowledge.

Barak's construction uses the technique which was presented by Feige, Lapidot, and Shamir in Ref. [25] and call it FLS paradigm. Two phases in the FLS technique will be combined together to obtain a ZKP. The first phase is called the generation phase, in which the prover and the verifier will generate a string. In the second phase, the prover proves to the verifier that either the theorem is true or that the generated string satisfies some property. The FLS technique is based on the notion of WI.

Barak's framework is described in Ref. [11]:

- Common input: x and a language L, such that $x \in L$, n is security parameter that makes sure that this protocol remains zero knowledge when executed up to n times concurrently.
- Auxiliary input to prover: w is a witness to the fact that $x \in L$.

1. *Phase*1 : *GenerationPhase*. The prover and the verifier engage in some protocol whose output is a string τ.
2. *Phase*2 : *WIProofPhase*. The prover proves to the verifier using a WI argument that it knows either a string w such that $(x, w) \in R$ or a string σ such that $(\tau, \sigma) \in S$. R and S are two statements based on language L that the prover wants to convince to the verifier. R is a binary relation that (x, w) is tested. $L(R) \overset{\text{def}}{=} \{x | \exists w \; s.t. \; (x, w) \in R\}$. It means that if $x \in L(R)$ and w is a string such that $(x, w) \in R$, then w is a witness for the fact that $x \in L(R)$. S is a binary relation that (τ, σ) is tested. $L(S) \overset{\text{def}}{=} \{\tau | \exists \sigma \; s.t. \; (\tau, \sigma) \in S\}$. Similarly, it means that σ is a witness for the fact that $\tau inL(S)$. More formally, the prover proves to the verifier using a WI proof knowledge that it knows a witness to the fact that $(x, \tau) \in L(S')$ where S' is defined so that $(x, \tau) \in L(S')$ if and only if there exists w' such that either $(x, w') \in R$ or $(\tau, w') \in S$.

2.10 Quality of ZKPs

The soundness condition is considered as a "security" property because it protects the verifier from adversarial behavior by the prover [17]. Usually, it has two commonly used versions:

- Statistical soundness: If $x \notin L$, then for all, even computationally unbounded, strategies P^*, V accepts in $(P^*, V)(x)$ with probability at most $1/3$. This gives rise to interactive proof systems.
- Computational soundness: If $x \notin L$, then for all polynomial-time strategies P^*, V accepts in $(P^*, V)(x)$ with probability at most $1/3$. This gives rise to interactive argument systems.

Zero knowledge is another "security" property, which protects the prover from leaking unnecessary information to the verifier. It comes in three versions of ZKPs based on three interpretations of "similarity."

1. The perfect zero-knowledge notion was suggested by Brassard and Crepeau [18]. The prover is restricted to polynomial time, while the verifier may have unlimited computing power. The computation simulating the actual interaction is identical to the original one.
2. Statistical zero knowledge requires that the computation simulating the actual interaction is statistically (e.g., in variation distance) close to the original one (with negligible error—smaller than any polynomial fraction in the length of common input) [7]. What is more, statistical zero knowledge requires that the zero-knowledge condition holds even for computationally unbounded verifier strategy V^*.

3. Computational (or rather general) zero knowledge requires that the transcript of the interaction is indistinguishable only under the computational complexity assumption, which means that no polynomial-time algorithm can distinguish the two distributions except with negligible probability. It only requires that the zero-knowledge condition hold for polynomial-time verifier strategy V^*.

The following definitions are from Ref. [19]. Let (A, B) be an interactive protocol. Let T, the transcript, be a random variable denoting the verifier view during the protocol on input x. That is, T is the sequence of messages between the prover and the verifier under the sequences of coin tosses for A and B. The string h denotes any private input that the verifier may have with the only restriction that its length is bounded by a polynomial in the length of the common input. $M(x, h)$ is distributed over the coin tosses of M on inputs x and h:

1. (A, B) is perfect zero knowledge for L if $\exists$ a probabilistic polynomial-time Turing machine M s.t. $\forall x \in L$, for all $a > 0$, for all strings h such that $|h| < |x|^a$, the random variable $M(x, h)$ and T are identically distributed.

2. (A, B) is statistically zero knowledge for L if $\exists$ a probabilistic polynomial-time Turing machine M s.t. $\forall x \in L$, for all $a > 0$, for all strings h such that $|h| < |x|^a$, for all constant $c > 0$ and sufficiently large $|x|$, $\sum_\alpha |prob\,(M\,(x, h) = \alpha) - prob(T = \alpha)| < \frac{1}{|x|^c}$

3. (A, B) is computationally zero knowledge for L if $\exists$ probabilistic polynomial-time Turing machine M s.t. $\forall$ polynomial-size circuit families $C = C_{|x|}$, $\forall$ constant a, $d > 0$, for all sufficiently large $|x|$ s.t. $x \in L$, and for all strings h such that $|h| < |x|^a$,

$$prob\left(C_{|x|}\,(\alpha) = 1 \mid \alpha \text{ random in } M(x, h)\right) - prob\left(C_{|x|}\,(\alpha)\right.$$
$$= 1 \mid \alpha \text{ random in } T\right) < \frac{1}{|x|^d}$$

Based on the two security conditions—soundness and zero knowledge that ZKPs have, we can obtain four kinds of ZKPs. They can be denoted as SZKP, CZKP, SZKA, and CZKA, in which the prefix of S indicates statistical and C indicates computational, while the suffix of P indicates interactive proofs (statistical soundness) and A indicates interactive arguments (computational soundness).

SZKPs are defined in the definition of zero knowledge that the distribution ensembles are required to be statistically indistinguishable rather than computationally indistinguishable. As far as security is concern,

SZKPs are of course the most attractive because the following several reasons [7]:

- SZKPs offer information-theoretic security to both parties. CZKPs only offer computational security to the prover, and SZKAs only offer computational security to the verifier. However, SZKPs hold their security properties regardless of the computational power of the verifier.
- SZKPs provide a clean model for the study of various questions regarding zero knowledge.
- SZKPs have some properties from a complexity theoretic point of view. It contains a number of specific problems believed to be hard such as graph nonisomorphism, graph isomorphism (GI), quadratic residuosity, and quadratic nonresiduosity, which are Karp reducible, and is closed under complementation.

Recalling the definition of zero knowledge, it is a CZKP rather than a SZKP because there do not exist commitment schemes that are simultaneously statistically hiding and statistically binding, which will be discussed in the next section. Under standard complexity assumptions, SZKA can also be constructed for every NP. The intractability assumption used for constructing SZKA for NP seems stronger than the assumption used for constructing CZKP for NP. Assuming both constructions exist, which is more preferable is more or less depending on the application: is it more important to protect the prover's secrets or to protect the verifier from being convinced of false assertions?

3. NP PROBLEM AND ZKPs

Complexity theory has an intriguing property that if any NP-complete problem has a polynomial-time solution, then every problem in NP has a polynomial-time solution.

Definition 2.5 (The Class NP) *NP is the class of decision problems X that admit a proof system $F \subseteq X \times Q$, s.t. there exists a polynomial $p(n)$ and a polynomial-time algorithm A such that [12]:*

1. *$\forall x \in X \exists q \in Q$ s.t. $(x, q) \in F$ and moreover, the size of q is at most $p(n)$, where n is the size of x.*
2. *For all pairs (x, q), algorithm A can verify whether or not $(x, q) \in F$.*

Definition 2.6 (Polynomial Reduction) *Let A and B be two problems. We say that A is polynomially Turing reducible to B if there exists an algorithm for* *solving A in a time that would be polynomial if we could solve arbitrary instances of problem B at unit cost [12].*

Definition 2.7 (NP–Complete Problem) *A decision problem X is NP complete if X ∈ NP and for every problem Y ∈ NP, Y is polynomially Turing reducible to X [12].*

It is not yet known if there are efficient solutions (polynomial time) to these problems in NP complete. Classic examples of these problems include satisfying a Boolean formula, the traveling salesman problem, the knapsack problem, and so on. But the validity of a proposed solution is easily tested. For example, consider the Hamiltonian cycle problem: it is hard to find an efficient algorithm to solve this problem, but it is very easy to verify if a sequence of nodes is a Hamiltonian cycle.

Assuming the existence of secure encryption functions, it has been shown that graph three colorability, which is known as a NP-complete problem, has a ZKP [6]. Since any problem in NP can be reduced to graph three colorability according to Karp [20], it ensures that any language in NP has associated with a ZKP system.

In the physical world, the secure encryption functions are represented by opaque, lockable boxes which are usually assumed to be available for the prover, and only the prover has the key. In order to implement the physical boxes algorithmically, a cryptographic primitive named "commitment scheme" [21] will be used. In ZKPs, the way of locking information is to "committing a secret bit" [22], which can be implemented by using any one–way function (assumed to exist).

This commitment scheme describes a two-stage protocol between the prover and the verifier [21]. In the first stage, the prover commits to a value *b*, which could be digital analogies of sealed envelopes (or, letter, locked boxes). This means sending the value to the verifier through binding some unique value without revealing the original value to the verifier (as when getting a locked box). This property is called hiding. The "hiding" property says that the verifier does not know anything about *b* during the commit stage. Later on, the prover "decommits" or "reveals" this value to the verifier. This means sending some auxiliary information that allows the verifier to read the uniquely committed value (as when sending the key to the lock) in order to assure that it is the original value. This property is called binding. The binding property means that after the commit stage, there is at most one value that the verifier can successfully open [23].

Recall that two security properties—hiding and binding—can be statistical (holding against computationally unbounded cheating strategies, except with negligible probability) or computational (holding against polynomial-time cheating strategies, except with negligible probability). It is impossible to achieve statistical security for both hiding and binding. But any one-way function could be used in the commitment scheme for statistical hiding or statistical binding.

The widely accepted theorem on how to construct CZKP system for any NP set was demonstrated by Goldreich, Micali, and Wigderson [6]. And the first construction of SZKA was given by Brassard *et al.* independently [24]. Feige *et al.* designed a ZKP on identification schemes in Ref. [25]. Constant-round ZKPs were first showed by Feige and Shamir [26].

4. ZKP APPLICATIONS

In this section, several problems are introduced with their ZKP construction. To provide a ZKP for a general NP statement, one can translate it into an instance of the graph three-colorability problem using a Karp reduction [20]. Another way to provide ZKPs avoiding a Karp reduction is using the simulation method after exploiting the properties of the specific NP-complete language.

4.1 ZKP for Graph Three Colorability

Definition 2.8 (Graph Three Colorability) *A graph $G(V, E)$ is said to be three colorable if there exists a mapping $\phi : V \rightarrow \{1, 2, 3\}$ (called a proper coloring) such that every two adjacent vertexes are assigned different colors (i.e., each $(u, v) \in E$ satisfies $\phi(u) = \phi(v)$). Such a three coloring induces a partition of the vertex set of the graph to three independent sets. The language graph three colorability, denoted G3C, consists of the set of undirected graphs that are three colorable.*

Figure 2.3 is a Peterson graph [27] with three colored vertices (red, green, and blue).

Suppose graph $G(V, E)$ is colored by ϕ ($\phi : V \rightarrow \{1, 2, 3\}$). Let $n = |V|$, $m = |E|$, and $S_3 = Sym\{1, 2, 3\}$. Since the graph is (simple and) connected, n and m are polynomially related (i.e., $n - 1 \leq m < n^2/2$).

Common input: A graph $G(V, E)$

The following four steps are executed m^2 times, each time using independent coin tosses [6]:

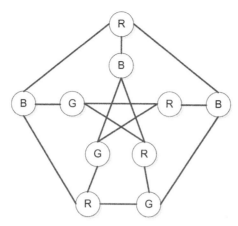

Figure 2.3 Three-colored graph.

1. P: The prover chooses at random an assignment of three colors to the three independent sets induced by ϕ, colors the graph using these three colors, and places these colors in n locked boxes each bearing the number of the corresponding vertex. More specifically, the prover chooses a permutation $\pi \in_R S_3$, places $\pi(\phi(i))$ in a box marked i ($\forall\, i \in V$), locks all boxes, and sends them (without the keys) to the verifier.

2. V: The verifier chooses at random an edge $e \in_R E$ and sends it to the prover. (Intuitively, the verifier asks to examine the colors of the endpoints of $e \in E$.)

3. P: If $e = (u, v) \in E$, then the prover sends the keys of u and v. Otherwise, the prover does nothing.

4. V: The verifier opens boxes u and v using the keys received and checks whether they contain two different elements of $\{1, 2, 3\}$. If the keys do not match the boxes, or the contents violate the condition, then the verifier rejects and stops. Otherwise, the verifier continues to the next iteration.

If the verifier has completed all m^2 iterations, then it accepts.

Figure 2.4 illustrates the ZKP for G3C.

This protocol constitutes a ZKP for G3C since it satisfies three properties.

* *Completeness*: If the graph is three colorable, then any pair of boxes u and v corresponding to some edge of the graph will certainly be colored differently. Therefore, an honest verifier will complete all m^2 iterations and accept with probability 1.

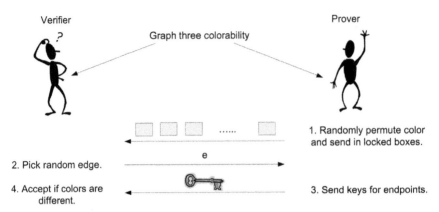

Figure 2.4 ZKP for G3C.

- *Soundness*: If the graph is not three colorable and the verifier follows the protocol, then no matter how the prover plays and at each round the verifier will reject with probability at least $\frac{1}{m}$. The probability that the verifier will accept is bounded by $\left(1 - \frac{1}{m}\right)^{m^2} \approx \exp(-m)$.

- *Zero knowledge*: The only information received by the verifier at each round is a pair of different randomly selected elements of $\{1, 2, 3\}$. It is crucial that the prover uses at each round an independently selected random permutation of the colors. Thus, the names of three classes at one round are uncorrelated to the names at another round.

4.2 ZKP for Feige–Fiat–Shamir Identification Scheme

The Feige–Fiat–Shamir identification scheme is one of the classic authentication zero-knowledge schemes [16]. The security of the Feige–Fiat–Shamir system is based on the fact that it is difficult to extract square roots modulo large composite integers of unknown factorization [12].

Initialization [28]:

1. A trusted center T selects and publishes an RSA (Ron Rivest, Adi Shamir and Leonard Adleman)-like modulus $n = pq$, but keeps the primes p and q secret.

2. The prover selects a secret s coprime to n, $1 \leq s \leq n - 1$, computes $v = s^2 \bmod n$, and registers v with T as her public key.

Identification Protocol [28]:

The following steps are executed t times, each time using independent random coin tosses:

1. P: The prover chooses a random r, $1 \leq r \leq n - 1$, and sends $x = r^2 \bmod n$ to the verifier.

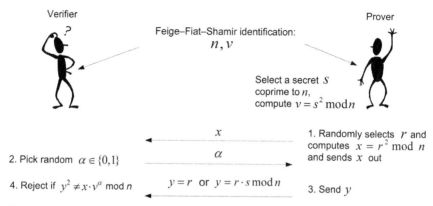

Figure 2.5 ZKP for Feige–Fiat–Shamir identification scheme.

2. V: The verifier randomly selects a bit $\alpha \in \{0, 1\}$ and sends α to the prover.
3. P: The prover computes and sends to the verifier y, where $y = r$ (if $\alpha = 0$), or $y = rs \bmod n$ (if $\alpha = 1$)
4. V: The verifier rejects if $y = 0$ or if $y^2 \neq x \cdot v^\alpha \bmod n$.

Figure 2.5 illustrates the ZKP for Feige–Fiat–Shamir identification scheme. If the verifier has completed all t iterations, then he accepts.

This protocol is a ZKP because it upholds the properties of completeness, soundness, and zero knowledge:

- *Completeness*: Suppose the prover possesses the secret s. Then she can always correctly provide the verifier with $y = r$ or $y = rs \bmod n$ upon request. Therefore, an honest verifier will complete all t iterations and accept with probability 1.
- *Soundness*: Suppose the prover does not possess the secret s. Then, during any given round, she can provide only one of $y = r$ or $y = rs \bmod n$. Therefore, an honest verifier will reject with probability $1/2$ in each round, so the probability the verifier will be fooled is 2^{-t}.
- *Zero knowledge*: The only information revealed in each round is $x = s^2 \bmod n$ and either $y = r$ or $y = rs \bmod n$. Such pairs (x, y) could be simulated by choosing y randomly and then define $x = y^2$ or $x = y^2/v$. Such pairs are computationally indistinguishable from the interaction with the prover.

4.3 ZKP for GI

The GI problem is basically asking the question: Given two graphs G_0 and G_1, is there a bijection between their sets of nodes that preserves edges?

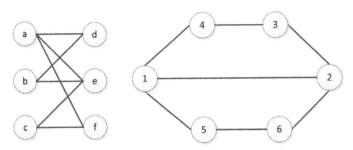

Figure 2.6 Graph isomorphism.

Definition 2.9 (Graph Isomorphism) *Two graphs $G(V, E)$ and $G'(V, E')$ are isomorphic if and only if there exists a permutation $\pi \in S_{|V|}$ (the symmetric group of $|V|$ elements) such that $(u, v) \in E$ iff $(\pi(u), \pi(v)) \in E'$. We can write $G' = \pi G$.*

There is an isomorphism between two graphs in Fig. 2.6. $f(a) = 1$, $f(b) = 6, f(c) = 3, f(d) = 5, f(e) = 2, f(f) = 4$.

The language GI consists of all the pairs of isomorphic graphs.

Common input: Two graphs $G_0(V, E)$ and $G_1(V, E')$. Let ϕ denote the isomorphism between G_0 and G_1, that is, $G_1 = \phi G_0$.

The following steps are executed t times, each time using independent random coin tosses [28]:

1. P: The prover generates a graph, H, which is a random isomorphic copy of G_1. This is done by selecting a permutation $\pi \in_R S_{|V|}$ and computing $H = \pi G_1$. The prover sends the graph H to the verifier.
2. V: The verifier chooses at random $\alpha \in_R \{0, 1\}$ and sends α to the prover.
3. P: If $\alpha = 1$, then the prover sends $\beta = \pi$ to the verifier, else ($\alpha = 0$) the prover sends $\beta = \pi \cdot \phi$. Here, $\pi \cdot \phi$ indicates the combination of π and ϕ.
4. V: If the permutation β received from the prover is not an isomorphism between G_α and H (i.e., $H \neq \beta G_\alpha$), then the verifier stops and rejects; otherwise, he continues.

Figure 2.7 illustrates the ZKP for GI.

If the verifier has completed t iterations of the above steps, then he accepts.

This protocol is a ZKP because it upholds the properties of completeness, soundness, and zero knowledge:

- *Completeness*: If $(G_0, G_1) \in GI$, then the random isomorphic copy H of G_1 will always be isomorphic to both G_0 and G_1. Therefore, an honest verifier will complete all iterations and accept with probability 1.

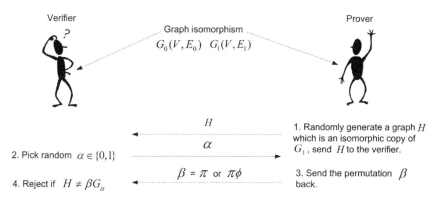

Figure 2.7 ZKP for graph isomorphism.

- *Soundness*: If $(G_0, G_1) \notin GI$, then the random isomorphic copy H of G_1 will be isomorphic to only one of G_0 or G_1. Therefore, an honest verifier will reject with probability $1/2$ in each round.
- *Zero knowledge*: The only information revealed in each round is either π or $\pi \cdot \phi$, where $\pi \in_R S_{|V|}$. Due to the random selection of π, a simulator which computes a random isomorphic copy of G_0 or G_1 or both is computationally indistinguishable from interaction with the prover.

4.4 ZKP for Hamiltonian Cycle [42]

Definition 2.10 (Hamiltonian Cycle) *Let G be a graph. A Hamiltonian cycle in G is a cycle that passes through all the nodes of G exactly once. The n nodes of G are labeled $N_1, N_2, \ldots, N_n$.*

Figure 2.8 has a Hamiltonian cycle labeled by the solid line.

The following protocol will be executed for k rounds.

1. P: The prover encrypts G with the boxes in secret by randomly mapping n labeled nodes $N_1, N_2, \ldots, N_n$ 1-1 into n labeled boxes $B_1, B_2, \ldots, B_n$ in such a way that each one of the $n!$ permutations of the nodes into the boxes is equally probable. For every pair of boxes (B_i, B_j) prepare a box labeled B_{ij}. This box is to contain a 1 if the node placed in B_i is adjacent to the node in B_j; 0 otherwise. All $(n + C_2^n)$ boxes are then to be locked and presented to the verifier.

2. V: Upon receiving $(n + C_2^n)$ boxes, the verifier has two choices:
   - $\alpha = 0$: The verifier can request that the prover unlock all the boxes. In this case, the verifier may check that the boxes contain a description of G. (For example, if N_1 is adjacent to both N_2, N_5 but no other nodes in G. If N_1 is in B_i, N_2 in B_j, and N_5 in B_k, then

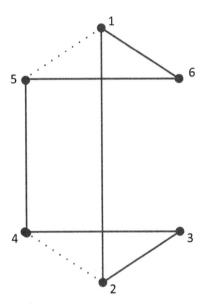

Figure 2.8 Hamiltonian cycle.

there should be a 1 in both B_{ij}, B_{ik}, and a 0 in B_{ix} for every other value of x.)

- $\alpha = 1$: The verifier can request that the prover open exactly n boxes $B_{ij}, B_{jk}, B_{kl} \ldots, B_{l'i}$, which can demonstrate that G contains a Hamiltonian cycle if all these boxes contain a 1. Since the B_i are not opened, the sequence of node numbers defining the Hamiltonian cycle in G is not revealed.

3. P: The prover opens the appropriate boxes according to one of the two random requests from the verifier (either the graph or the Hamiltonian cycle).

4. V: The verifier accepts the proof if the prover complies and rejects otherwise.

Figure 2.9 illustrates the ZKP for Hamiltonian cycle.

This protocol is a ZKP because it upholds the properties of completeness, soundness, and zero knowledge.

- *Completeness*: If the prover knows the graph, G, contains a Hamiltonian cycle, he can successfully show the graph or cycle according to the requests from the verifier. So the verifier will complete all k rounds and accept with probability 1.

- *Soundness*: If the graph does not contain a Hamiltonian cycle, the prover's probability of convincing the verifier that he does know the

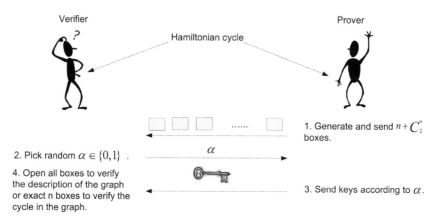

Figure 2.9 ZKP for Hamiltonian cycle.

graph contains a Hamiltonian cycle is $1/2$ in each round. His probability of convincing the verifier that he does know is $\leq 1/2^k$ when there are k rounds.

- *Zero knowledge*: In each round, the verifier either obtains an encrypted graph of G or a random n cycle. When the prover reveals all the boxes that describe the G, it is only one of the $n!$ random mappings of the n nodes of G into the n labeled boxes. When the prover reveals the boxes containing a cycle, it is just a random n cycle. Thus, the verifier gets no useful information.

4.5 Another ZKP for Graph Three Colorability [42]

The n nodes of G are labeled $N_1, N_2, \ldots, N_n$. Suppose the graph is colored with red, white, and blue. If node N_i is colored red, it is called N_i^R.

1. P: The prover prepares $3n$ pairs of boxes $\langle B_1^c, B_1 \rangle, \langle B_2^c, B_2 \rangle, \ldots,$ $\langle B_{3n}^c, B_{3n} \rangle$. Without revealing to the verifier, the prover randomly maps $3n$ nodes $N_1^R, \ldots, N_n^R, N_1^W, \ldots, N_n^W, N_1^B, \ldots, N_n^B$ 1-1 into the $3n$ pairs of boxes. Each of the $(3n)!$ permutations mapping the $\{N_i^x\}$ onto the $\langle B_j^c, B_j \rangle$ is equally probable. The prover puts x (the color) into B_j^c and puts i (the node number) into B_j. For every pair of number-containing boxes (B_i, B_j), prepare a box labeled B_{ij}. This box contains 1 if the node of G in B_i has the color B_i^c, if the node of G in B_j has the color $B_j^{c'}$, and if the node in B_i is adjacent in G to the node in B_j and contains 0 otherwise. All boxes are then locked and presented to the verifier.

2. **V:** Upon receiving $(2 \cdot 3n + C_2^n)$ boxes, the verifier has two choices:

   a. The verifier can request that the prover unlock all the boxes B_{ij} and all the numbers containing boxes B_i, but none of the colors containing B_i^c. In this way, the prover reveals the graph G without revealing its coloring. The verifier can check that the boxes contain a correct description of G.

   b. The verifier can request that the prover open the $3n$ boxes $\{B_i^c\}$ to reveal the colors they contain, and then open just those boxes B_{ij} such that B_i^c contains the same color as B_j^c. The opened boxes B_{ij} will all contain a 0 if and only if any two nodes that are colored the same are not adjacent in the graph represented by the boxes. The verifier can check the correct three coloring.

3. **P:** The prover opens the appropriate boxes according to one of the two random requests from the verifier (either all boxes without colors or adjacent vertices with different colors).

4. **V:** The verifier accepts the proof if the prover complies and rejects otherwise.

This protocol is a ZKP because it upholds the properties of completeness, soundness, and zero knowledge:

- *Completeness*: If the graph is three colorable, those nodes that are colored the same are not adjacent in graph. So the verifier will complete all rounds and accept with probability 1.

- *Soundness*: If the graph is not three-colorable, the prover's probability of convincing the verifier that he does know the graph is three colorable is $1/2$ in each round. His chance of convincing the verifier that he does know is $\leq 1/2^k$ when there are k rounds.

- *Zero knowledge*: In each round, the verifier obtains either an encrypted graph or boxes containing "0." When the prover reveals all the boxes that describe the graph, it is only one of the random mappings of the n nodes of graph into n labeled boxes. When the prover reveals the boxes containing "0," the verifier gets no useful information without the corresponding numbers of nodes.

4.6 ZKP Sketch for SAT

The quadratic residuosity problem is the question of distinguishing by calculating the quadratic residues modulo n, where n is a composite number of two odd primes p and q. Under the assumption of quadratic residuosity that two states are computationally indistinguishable through the calculation of the quadratic residues modulo n, a protocol for satisfiability (SAT) is suggested that directly simulates a circuit that evaluates given instances of SAT [29].

The general technique in Ref. [18] is through the simulation of an arbitrary Boolean circuit without disclosing the inputs or any intermediary results. At the end of the protocol, if the final output of the circuit is 1, then the circuit is satisfiable, but nothing else.

Let $u = b_1, b_2, \ldots, b_k$ be a k bit string of the prover. For each $1 \le i \le k$, let z_i and z'_i be the two encryptions of b_i randomly chosen by the prover. It is easy for the prover to convince the verifier that the k bit strings encrypted by $z_1, z_2, \ldots, z_k$ and $z'_1, z'_2, \ldots, z'_k$ are identical without providing the verifier with any additional information by the following string equality protocol.

Definition 2.11 (String Equality Protocol) *For each i, $1 \le i \le k$, the prover gives the verifier some $x_i \in \mathbb{Z}^*_{\times}$ (denoting the set of integers relatively prime to n between 1 and $n - 1$) so that $z_i z'_i \equiv x_i^2 (mod \ n)$.*

Definition 2.12 (Boolean Computation Protocol) *Consider any Boolean function $B : \{0, 1\}^t \to \{0, 1\}$ agreed upon between the prover and the verifier, and any bits $b_1, b_2, \ldots, b_t$ only known to the prover. For $1 \le i \le t$, let z_i be an encryption of b_i known to the verifier. Let $b = B(b_1, b_2, \ldots, b_t)$. The prover produces an encryption z for b and convinces the verifier that z encrypts the correct bit without giving the verifier any information on the input bits $b_1, b_2, \ldots, b_t$ nor on the result b.*

A permuted truth table for the Boolean function B is introduced here, which is a binary string of length $(t + 1)2^t$ formed of 2^t blocks of $t + 1$ bits. The last bit of each block is the value of B on the other t bits of the block. Let s be the number of permutations agreed upon between the prover and the verifier:

1. P: The prover randomly chooses s permuted truth tables for B and discloses encryptions for each of them.
2. V: The verifier selects a random subset $X \subseteq \{1, 2, \ldots, s\}$ and sends it to the prover as a challenge.
3. P: The prover chooses one of the following options based on the request from the verifier:
   - For each $j \in X$, the prover opens the entire encryption of the jth permuted truth table.
   - For each $j \notin X$, the prover points to the appropriate block in the encryption of the jth permuted truth table and uses the following

string equality protocol to convince the verifier that $z_1, z_2, \ldots, z_t z$ encrypts the same bit string as this block.

4. V: The verifier makes the following verifications:
- The verifier checks if it is a valid truth table for B.
- The verifier checks if $z_1, z_2, \ldots, z_t z$ encrypts the same bit string.

Figure 2.10 illustrates the ZKP for Boolean computation.

Based on the above discussions, a ZKP sketch has been designed for SAT. $f : \{0, 1\}^k \rightarrow \{0, 1\}$ is the function computed by some satisfiable Boolean formula for which the prover knows that there is an assignment $b_1, b_2, \ldots, b_k \in \{0, 1\}$ so that $f(b_1, b_2, \ldots, b_k) = 1$. Assume that the Boolean formula is given using arbitrary unary and binary Boolean operators. The prover will produce encryptions $z_1, z_2, \ldots, z_k$ of $b_1, b_2, \ldots, b_k$. Then, the prover will guide the verifier through the encrypted evaluation of the formula, using the Boolean computation protocol, one Boolean operator at a time. The result will be a z which is the encryption for the value of $f(b_1, b_2, \ldots, b_k)$. Then, the prover opens z and shows the verifier that it encrypts a 1.

4.7 ZKP for Circuit Computations

In Ref. [29], it is possible to directly simulate the computation of any given computational device. Simulation is used to separate the data encryption from the encryption of the device's structural (or control) information. It directly proves the result of the computation, avoiding the Karp reduction from a specific NP-complete problem.

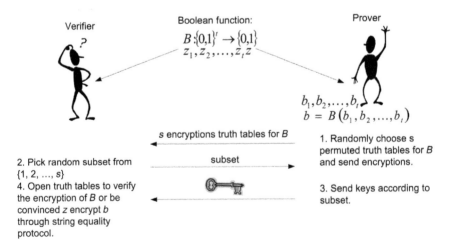

Figure 2.10 ZKP for Boolean computation.

In the protocol, the essential idea is that the prover constructs and sends to the verifier a copy of a simulation of the computing device. This copy should include encoding of the possible input, intermediate results, and output data. In addition, it includes encoding of structural information about the computing device. Upon receiving the encoding information, the verifier chooses a bit $\alpha \in \{0, 1\}$ and sends it back.

- With probability $1/2$, the verifier decides to verify, that is, to request that the prover open all the encryptions in the copy. In this way, the verifier can check if the construction is a legal one with the correct structural information.
- With probability $1/2$, the verifier chooses to compute, in which case the prover opens only the result of the computation. In order to prove that the output presented is in fact the computed result, the prover opens only parts that are involved in the computation, while other information is left encrypted. The unopened information appears random.

The process is repeated r times; each time the verifier either chooses to verify or chooses to compute. If all verifications are successful, and all the computations produce a connection to the same opened output, then the verifier accepts the result of the computation.

The prover uses an encryption procedure E and simulates the computation of a circuit C in a minimum-knowledge fashion with the verifier. Let E(C) denote the encryption:

1. P: The prover probabilistically encrypts C using an encryption procedure E. Then, the prover sends E(C) to the verifier.
2. V: The verifier chooses a bit $\alpha \in \{0, 1\}$ and sends it back.
3. P: The prover chooses one of the corresponding actions based on the requests from the verifier:
   - $\alpha = 0$ {verify}: The prover opens all the encryptions of all gates in E(C) and sends the cleartext circuit to the verifier
   - $\alpha = 1$ {compute}: The prover opens only the pointers of the specific computation and sends the cleartexts of these pointers to the verifier including the outputs.
4. V: The verifier does the corresponding verifications:
   - $\alpha = 0$: the verifier verifies that C is properly encrypted;
   - $\alpha = 1$: the verifier verifies that the opened pointers lead from the (unopened) input entries to the output pointers.

Figure 2.11 illustrates the ZKP for circuit computation.

If all computations give the same value and all verifications are successful, then the verifier accepts. Otherwise, the verifier rejects.

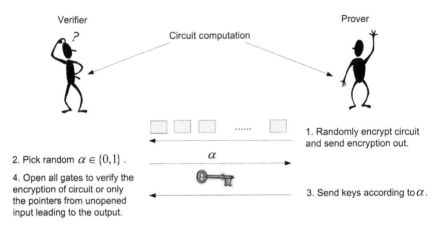

Figure 2.11 ZKP for circuit computation.

4.8 ZKP for Exact Cover

Definition 2.13 (Exact Cover) *A set* $\{u_i, \ i = 1, \ 2, \dots, t\}$. *A family* $\{S_j\}$ *is a subset of the set* $\{u_i, \ i = 1, \ 2, \dots, t\}$. *Exact cover means that there is a subfamily* $\{T_h\} \subseteq \{S_j\}$, *such that sets* T_h *are disjoint and* $\bigcup T_h = \bigcup S_j = \{u_i, \ i = 1, 2, \dots, t\}$.

The following protocol will be executed for t rounds. The verifier uses a coin toss in each round:

Let $|T_h| = m$, $|S_j| = n$.

1. P: The prover prepares the following four kinds of boxes:
   - t labeled boxes $B_1, B_2, \dots, B_t$ which will contain set $\{u_i, \ i = 1, 2, \dots, t\}$ in a random order
   - n labeled boxes $A_1, A_2, \dots A_n$ which will contain an element in S_j
   - $n \cdot t$ black boxes in a matrix as follows: if the set member in B_i is in the S_j of A_j, then insert a 1; otherwise insert a 0.

$$
\begin{array}{cccccc}
 & B_1 & B_2 & B_3 & \dots\dots & B_t \\
A_1 & 1 & 0 & 0 & \dots\dots & 0 \\
A_2 & 0 & 0 & 1 & \dots\dots & 0 \\
\dots & 0 & 1 & 0 & \dots\dots & 0 \\
\dots & 0 & 0 & 0 & \dots & 1 \quad 0 \\
A_n & 1 & 0 & 0 & \dots\dots & 1
\end{array}
$$

   - For every two rows in matrix, a pair of boxes is prepared as ⟨*IndexIndex, Result*⟩. The first box contains indexes of two rows. The second box contains the product operation of any two row vectors (one is row vector and the other is the transpose of row vector). If the result of product operation is 0, $Result = 0$; otherwise, $Result = 1$.

2. V: Upon receiving $(2 \cdot t + n \cdot t + 2 \cdot C_2^n)$ black boxes, the verifier has two choices:

   - $\alpha = 0$: The verifier can ask to open all the boxes to verify if the description of the problem is correct.
   - $\alpha = 1$: The verifier asks the prover to open some pairs of boxes with $Result = 0$. With the index showing in these boxes, the verifier also asks to open the corresponding row in the matrix to check if $\bigcup T_h = \bigcup S_j = \{u_i, \ i = 1, \ 2, \ \ldots, t\}$.)

3. P: The prover opens the appropriate boxes according to the two random requests from the verifier (either all the boxes describing the exact cover problem or disjoint solution sets).

4. V: The verifier accepts the proof if the prover complies and rejects otherwise.

Figure 2.12 illustrates the ZKP for exact cover.

This protocol is a ZKP because it upholds the properties of completeness, soundness, and zero knowledge:

- *Completeness*: If the prover knows the exact cover, he can encrypt the correct information in the matrix. So the verifier will complete all rounds and accept with probability 1.
- *Soundness*: If the prover does not know the exact cover, the prover's chance of convincing the verifier that he does know the exact cover is $1/2$ in each round: either the exact cover problem is correctly encrypted, or there are disjoint solution sets. His chance of convincing

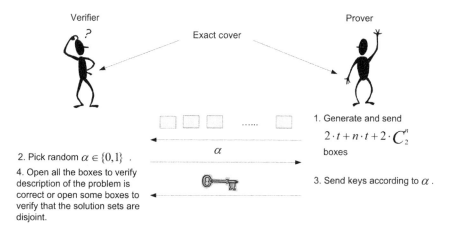

Figure 2.12 ZKP for exact cover

the verifier that he does know the exact cover is $\leq 1/2^k$ when there are k rounds.

- *Zero knowledge*: In each round, the verifier either obtains a random matrix with "0" and "1" or obtains one element in set $\{S_j\}$ which is known to the verifier beforehand. Thus, there is no useful information transferred.

An example will be used to illustrate ZKP for exact cover, suppose: $S = \{A, B, C, D, E, F\}$. $\{u_i\} = \{1, 2, 3, 4, 5, 6, 7\}$. $A = \{1, 4, 7\}, B = \{1, 4\}, C = \{4, 5, 6\}, D = \{3, 5, 6\}, E = \{2, 3, 5, 6\}, F = \{2, 7\}$.

In ZKP for exact cover, the prover will prepare seven black boxes named $B_1, B_2, \ldots, B_7$, which will contain elements in $\{u_i\}$ in a random order. Additional six black boxes named $A_1, A_2, \ldots, A_6$ will be used to contain sets in $\{S_i\}$. With A_i, B_i, the following matrix will be prepared:

$$
\begin{array}{ccccccc}
2 & 1 & 6 & 5 & 3 & 7 & 4 \\
B_1 & B_2 & B_3 & B_4 & B_5 & B_6 & B_7
\end{array}
$$

$S_6 A_1$	1	0	0	0	0	1	0
$S_1 A_2$	0	1	0	0	0	1	1
$S_4 A_3$	0	0	1	1	1	0	0
$S_2 A_4$	0	1	0	0	0	0	1
$S_3 A_5$	0	0	1	1	0	0	1
$S_5 A_6$	1	0	1	1	1	0	0

The prover also prepares the following pairs (Table 2.1) of boxes which contain indexes and result of $*$ operation of any two rows:

The prover will send all of those black boxes to the verifier. Upon receiving $(2 \cdot 7 + 6 \cdot 7 + 2 \cdot 15) = 86$ black boxes, the verifier has two choices:

- The verifier asks the prover to open all black boxes to verify if the boxes contain the public exact cover problem.
- The verifier asks the prover to open some pair of boxes with *Result* $= 0$. The prover will open $(13, 0)$ and $(34, 0)$. With indexes 1, 3, and 4, the verifier ask the prover to open rows 1, 3 and 4 in the matrix and check if elements in rows 1, 3, and 4 are combined together, covering all elements in the set $\{u_i\}$.

Table 2.1 Black Boxes for Index and Product Operation

$1*2, 1$	$1*3, 0$	$1*4, 0$	$1*5, 1$	$1*6, 1$
$2*3, 0$	$2*4, 1$	$2*5, 1$	$2*6, 0$	$3*4, 0$
$3*5, 0$	$3*6, 1$	$4*5, 1$	$4*6, 0$	$5*6, 1$

4.9 ZKP for 0–1 Knapsack

Definition 2.14 (0–1 Knapsack) *There are n kinds of items. Each kind of item i has a value v_i and a weight w_i. The maximum weight that a bag can carry is W. The 0–1 knapsack algorithm determines the subsets of items which give maximum value without exceeding the maximum weight of the bag. Mathematically, the 0–1 knapsack problem can be formulated as*

- *Maximize $\sum_i^n v_i \cdot x_i$ with $x_i \in \{0, 1\}$*
- *Subject to $\sum_i^n w_i \cdot x_i \leq W$ with $x_i \in \{0, 1\}$*

The simple case of the problem with the property that for each kind of item the weight equals the value $w_i = v_i$ is as follows:

The 0–1 simple knapsack problem is to find a binary n-vector x such that a given W equals to $w \cdot x$. A supposed solution x is easily checked in at most n additions, but finding a solution is believed to belong to *NPC*. As n is larger than 100 or 200, the number of operations grows exponentially and computationally infeasible for exhaustive trial-and-error search over all 2^n possible x.

However, the degree of difficulty is crucially dependent on the choice of w. If $w = (1, 2, 4, \ldots, 2^n)$, then solving for x is equivalent to finding the binary representation of W. Generally, if for all i, $w_i > \sum_{j=1}^{i-1} w_j$, then x is also easily found. $x_n = 1$ if and only if $W \geq w_n$ and for $i = n - 1$, $n - 2, \ldots, 1$, $x_i = 1$ if and only if $W - \sum_{j=i+1}^{n} x_j \cdot w_j \geq w_i$. A trapdoor knapsack is defined as one in which carefully choice of w as above. They form a proper subset of all possible knapsacks, and their solutions are not as difficult as the hardest knapsacks in NP theory [30]. In this paper, we are not considering trapdoor knapsacks.

According to the Karp's reduction theorem, the ZKP for knapsack problem can be generated in a similar way as the ZKP for exact cover problem.

The following protocol will be executed for t rounds. The verifier uses a coin toss in each round.

1. P: The prover prepares the following four kinds of boxes:
   - n labeled boxes $B_1, B_2, \ldots, B_n$ which will contain items $w_1, w_2, \ldots, w_n$ in a random order
   - m boxes $S_1, S_2, \ldots, S_m$ will contain some numbers which are summation of random items from w_i
   - $m \cdot n$ black boxes in a matrix as follows: if the item B_i is included in sum S_i, then insert a 1; otherwise insert a 0:

$$
\begin{array}{l}
B_1\ B_2\ B_3\ \ldots\ldots\ B_n \\
S_1\ \ 1\ \ 0\ \ 0\ \ldots\ldots\ 0 \\
S_2\ \ 0\ \ 0\ \ 1\ \ldots\ldots\ 0 \\
\ldots\ \ 0\ \ 1\ \ 0\ \ldots\ldots\ 0 \\
\ldots\ \ 0\ \ 0\ \ 0\ \ldots\ 1\ \ 0 \\
S_m\ 1\ \ 0\ \ 0\ \ldots\ldots\ 1
\end{array}
$$

- For every two rows in matrix, a pair of boxes is prepared as ⟨*Index* ∗ *Index*, *Result*⟩. The first box contains indexes of two rows. The second box contains the product operation of any two row vectors (one is row vector and the other is the transpose of row vector). If the result of product operation is 0, *Result* = 0; otherwise, *Result* = 1.

2. V: Upon receiving $(2 \cdot n + m \cdot n + 2 \cdot C_2^m)$ black boxes, the verifier has two choices:
   - $\alpha = 0$: The verifier asks the prover to open all the boxes to verify if they are satisfied the original simple knapsack problem.
   - $\alpha = 1$: The verifier asks the prover to open a subset of the summation boxes S_i with $\sum S_i = W$. The verifier also asks to open all the pairs of boxes to check if *Result* = 0 within the subset of S_i.

3. P: The prover opens the appropriate boxes according to the two random requests from the verifier (either all the boxes describing the knapsack problem or those boxes where W is equal to some summation S_i with *Result* = 0 for each pair).

4. V: The verifier accepts the proof if the prover complies and rejects otherwise.

Figure 2.13 illustrates the ZKP for 0–1 simple knapsack. If the verifier has completed t iterations of the above steps, then he accepts.

This protocol is a ZKP because it upholds the properties of completeness, soundness, and zero knowledge:

- *Completeness*: If the prover knows the solution to the simple knapsack, he can encrypt the correct information in all the boxes. So the verifier will complete all rounds and accept with probability 1.
- *Soundness*: If the prover does not know the solution to the simple knapsack, the prover's chance of convincing the verifier that he does know the solution is 1/2 in each round: either the simple knapsack problem or some summation equal to constraint W. His chance of convincing the verifier that he does know the exact cover is $\leq 1/2^k$ when there are k rounds.

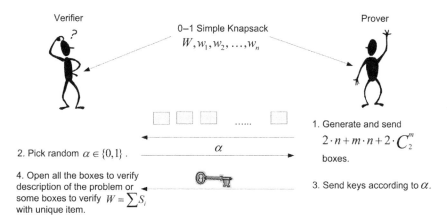

Verifier

0–1 Simple Knapsack
$W, w_1, w_2, \ldots, w_n$

Prover

$\square \ \square \ \square \quad \ldots\ldots \quad \square$

2. Pick random $\alpha \in \{0, 1\}$.

α

1. Generate and send
$2 \cdot n + m \cdot n + 2 \cdot C_2^m$
boxes.

4. Open all the boxes to verify
description of the problem or
some boxes to verify $W = \sum S_i$
with unique item.

3. Send keys according to α.

Figure 2.13 ZKP for 0–1 simple knapsack.

- *Zero knowledge*: In each round, the verifier either obtains a random matrix with "0" and "1" or obtains some random numbers. Thus, there is no useful information transferred.

5. ADVANCED TOPICS IN COMPOSING ZKPs

5.1 Composing ZKPs

ZKPs have many applications in cryptographic areas such as identity verification, authentication, and key exchange. Provided that one-way functions exist, ZKPs can be used to force parties to behave according to a predetermined protocol, such as multiparty secure computations [31]. The next natural question is whether the zero-knowledge condition is preserved under a variety of composition operations: sequential, parallel, and concurrent. This question not only belongs to the theoretical area but also is crucial to the application of ZKPs in the cryptographic area. For example, we want to make sure that the information obtained by the verifier during the execution of a ZKP will not enable him to extract any additional knowledge from subsequent executions of the same protocol.

For $T \in \{$*sequential, parallel, concurrent*$\}$, a protocol is T-zero knowledge if it is zero knowledge under a composition of type T [7]. The definitions of T-zero knowledge are derived by considering that the verifiers can initiate a polynomial number of interactions with the prover using scheduling type T.

Protocol repetition, which repeats the basic protocol many times independently and links them together, is mainly used for error reduction.

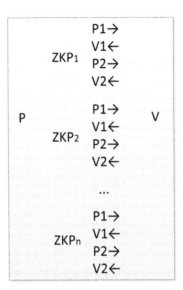

Figure 2.14 Sequential composition of ZKP.

Protocol composition is different than protocol repetition; the prover is not assumed to coordinate its actions between different executions of the protocol [32]. If the verifier has some misbehavior in protocol repetition, the prover can refuse to continue execution. By contrast, in protocol composition, the prover is still obligated to continue interaction with other executions of the protocol. The obvious way to perform repetition would be to execute the basic protocol sequentially, but it suffers from a high round complexity, resulting in a high number of message exchanges in the execution. Parallel repetition that conducts the basic protocol in parallel is used as a way of decreasing the error probability while maintaining the number of rounds of message:

1. In sequential composition, the ZKP is invoked (polynomially) many times, where each invocation follows the termination of the previous one [7]. Assuming a basic ZKP contains four-round $P1, V1, P2, V2$ message passing, Fig. 2.14 shows the sequential composition. It is the most basic case of protocol composition. Every protocol that is zero knowledge is sequential-zero-knowledge, which means that zero knowledge is closed under sequential composition.

2. In parallel composition, (polynomially) many instances of the ZKP are invoked at the same time and proceed at the same pace [7]. Under the assumption of a synchronous model of communication, the executions are totally synchronized so that the ith messages in all instances are sent

i	ZKP$_1$	ZKP$_2$		ZKP$_n$
1	P1$\rightarrow$	P1$\rightarrow$	...	P1$\rightarrow$
2	V1$\leftarrow$	V1$\leftarrow$	...	V1$\leftarrow$
3	P2$\rightarrow$	P2$\rightarrow$	...	P2$\rightarrow$
4	V2$\leftarrow$	v2$\leftarrow$	...	V2$\leftarrow$

(P ... V)

Figure 2.15 Parallel composition of ZKP.

exactly at the same time. As shown in Fig. 2.15, assuming a basic ZKP contains four-round $P1(i = 1), V1(i = 2), P2(i = 3), V2(i = 4)$ message passing, the ith message in all ZKPs should be sent out at the same time.

Goldreich and Krawczyk [14] presented a simple protocol that is zero knowledge, but is not closed under parallel composition. The example is described in Table 2.2:

The prover's strategy is zero knowledge because:

- If the verifier chooses 0, then it is infeasible for the verifier to guess a passing pair (β, γ) since the α is randomly chosen by the prover. The verifier does not obtain anything from the interaction.
- If the verifier chooses 1, then it obtains a pair $(\beta, f(\alpha\beta))$. Since β is selected by the prover, for any α, the value $f(\alpha\beta))$ is random to the verifier and $(\beta, f(\alpha\beta))$ is indistinguishable from a uniformly selected pair of n-bit long strings.

However, if the verifier conducts two concurrent executions with the prover, there will be information leakage, illustrated in Table 2.3. In this case, the verifier chooses 0 in one session and 1 in another session. Upon receiving the prover's message α in the first session, the verifier sends α as its own message in the second session and obtains a pair $(\beta, f(\alpha\beta))$ from

Table 2.2 Protocol not Closed Under Parallel Composition

Consider the prover holding a secret and a random function $f : \{0, 1\}^{2n} \rightarrow \{0, 1\}^n$ and willing to participate in the protocol. The verifier is supposed to send the prover a binary value $\{0, 1\}$:

For choice 0, the prover uniformly selects $\alpha \in \{0, 1\}^n$ and sends it to the verifier which is supposed to reply with a pair of n-bit long strings, denoted (β, γ). The prover checks whether or not $f(\alpha\beta) = \gamma$. The input of f function, $\alpha\beta$, is the concatenation operation of two n-bit string. If the equality is satisfied, the prover sends the verifier the secret he has.

For choice 1, the verifier is supposed to uniformly select $\alpha \in \{0, 1\}^n$ and send it to the prover, which selects uniformly $\beta \in \{0, 1\}^n$ and replies with the pair $(\beta, f(\alpha\beta))$.

Table 2.3 Parallel Composition Leads to Information Leakage

$V = 0$	$V = 1$
$P \xrightarrow{\alpha} V$	
	$P \xleftarrow{\alpha} V$
	$P \xrightarrow{(\beta, f(\alpha\beta))} V$
$P \xleftarrow{(\beta, \gamma)} V$	
$P \xrightarrow{secret} V \ (f(\alpha\beta) == \gamma)$	

the prover's execution of the second session. Then, the verifier sends the pair $(\beta, f(\alpha\beta))$ to the first session of the prover, which will satisfy the equation $f(\alpha\beta) = \gamma$, and the verifier will obtain the desired secret.

Based on the above example, zero knowledge is not closed under parallel composition in general [32]. However, assuming that one-way functions exist, it has been proved that there exist zero-knowledge protocols for NP that are closed under parallel composition and having a constant number of rounds [33]. Conceptually, the independently execution of one basic protocol will give no information to other execution of basic protocol since the prover will respond independently based on the message from each execution.

Using a simulator is the technique to demonstrate the zero-knowledge property. The idea behind it is that whatever the verifier might have learned from interacting with the prover, the verifier could learn by himself by running the simulator. The simulator has two advantages over the prover to compensate for not knowing the secret as the prover does [11]. The first advantage is that the simulator knows and can determine the questions the verifier will ask. The second advantage is that the simulator has many choices to answer the verifier's questions. After it fails to answer a question from the verifier, the simulator simply chooses not to output this interaction and goes back to some point to output only the successful interaction. This process is called rewind which helps the simulator to rewind back from the failure and try again. The black-box simulator, which simulates the interacting of the prover with the verifier without access to the strategy of that verifier, is used to demonstrate the zero knowledge [33].

3. Concurrent composition is a more general protocol composition, which was first considered by Dwork *et al.* [34]. Here, (polynomially) many instances of the protocol are invoked at an arbitrary time and proceed at an arbitrary pace [7]. This allows one or multiple verifiers to engage in

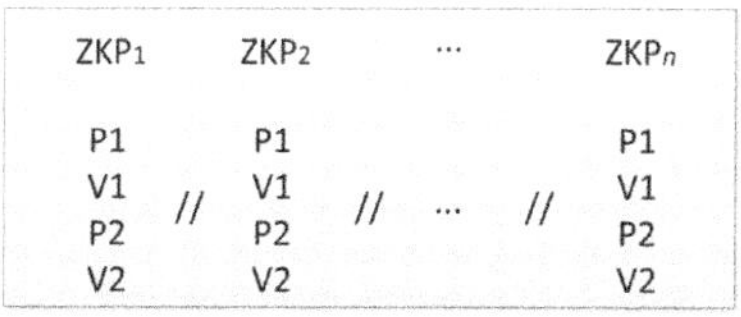

Figure 2.16 Concurrent composition of ZKP.

many proofs with the prover and arbitrarily interleave the messages by running some of the protocols ahead in order to gain information that will enable it to attack some of the other protocols. Within each proof, the verifier must follow the proper order of the steps. Among different proofs, the verifier can interleave arbitrarily. For example, the verifier may execute the first step of proof 1 and then execute all steps of proof 2 in order to obtain some knowledge in advance to execute the remaining steps in proof 1. Concurrent composition is shown in Fig. 2.16.

There are two models of concurrent composition: a purely asynchronous model and an asynchronous model with timing. The purely asynchronous model is a simpler model and requires no assumptions about the underlying communication channels. While an asynchronous model with timing, each party is assumed to hold a local clock such that the relative clock rates are bounded by an *a priori* known constant.

The timing model assumes that each party holds a local clock such that the relative clock rates are bounded by an *a priori* known constant [34]. There are two constants involved in the timing assumption: ρ and Δ. ρ is a global time bound on the relative rates of the local clock and is known to all parties. Δ is an upper bound on the message handling and delivery time. Under this timing model, a constant-round concurrent ZKP can be constructed as shown in Ref. [34].

Some problems will arise if time-driven operations are considered. The use of time-driven operations, such as timeout of incoming messages, receipt, and delay of outgoing messages, will slow down the execution of the protocol. However, in the absence of more appealing alternatives, the use of this timing model still is considered reasonable [7].

5.1.1 The Richardson–Kilian Concurrent ZKP Protocol

Under standard intractability assumptions, concurrent ZKPs exist for NP in a purely asynchronous model by Richardson and Kilian (RK) [35]. In this model, a verifier is allowed to run up to k interactive proofs with the prover. The RK protocol consists of two stages: an $O(k)$ preamble messages and a main body. The first stage is independent of the common input, in which

Table 2.4 RK Protocol

First stage
$V \rightarrow P$: Commit to $v_1, v_2, \ldots, v_k$
For $j = 1, 2, \ldots, k$
$P \rightarrow V$: Commit to p_j
$V \rightarrow P$: Decommit to v_j

Second stage
$P \leftrightarrow V$: Zero-knowledge proof for statement is true or $\exists j$ s.t. $v_j = p_j$

the verifier and the prover will be engaged in $O(k)$ message exchanges. First, the verifier commits to k random n-bit strings $v_1, v_2, \ldots, v_k \in \{0, 1\}^n$, where n is the security parameter of the protocol that represents the number of concurrent executions and k is the parameter that determines the number of rounds. In the following k iterations between the prover and the verifier, the prover commits to a random n-bit string, p_j, and the verifier decommits to the corresponding v_j. In the second stage, the prover provides proof either for the statement is true or for some $j \in \{1, 2, \ldots, k\}$ $v_j = p_j$. Table 2.4 illustrates two stages.

The technique used here is from WI in Section 2.7: instead of proving a statement T, the prover proves a weaker theorem $T \vee W$, where W is a statement that will fail with extremely high probability [35]. In the actual interactions, there is little chance for the prover to guess v_j from the verifier. Thus, the prover has no choice but to provide the proof for the statement T.

It is necessary to examine whether the zero-knowledge property is still preserved in the protocol. Recall that in order to demonstrate the zero-knowledge property, a simulator has to be generated that can simulate the views of every polynomial-time adversary interacting with the prover. Under concurrent composition, the simulator's task becomes more complicated [32]. In the RK protocol, the preamble messages will be used by the simulator to its advantage. Whenever the simulator may cause $v_j = p_j$ to happen for some j, it can simulate the rest of the protocol and provide a WI proof. The larger the number of rounds in the preamble, the more resistant the result is to concurrent attacks, and the easier the simulation task is. However, the number of rounds in the protocol will also increase.

5.1.2 The Improved Concurrent ZKP Protocol
Prabhakharan, Rosen, and Sahai (PRS) proposed a more sophisticated concurrent ZKP in Ref. [36] with $O(\alpha(n) \cdot logn)$ rounds of iteration, where $\alpha(\cdot)$ is any super-constant function such as *loglogn*. The PRS protocol also

Table 2.5 PRS Protocol

First stage

$V \to P$: Commit to σ, $\{\sigma^0_{i,j}\}^k_{i,j=1}$, $\{\sigma^1_{i,j}\}^k_{i,j=1}$, for each i,j, $\sigma^0_{i,j} \oplus \sigma^1_{i,j} = \sigma$

For $j = 1, 2, \ldots, k$:

$P \to V$: Send k-bit string $r_j = r_{1,j}, r_{2,j}, \ldots, r_{k,j}$

$V \to P$: Decommit k strings of $\sigma^{r_{1,j}}_{1,j}, \sigma^{r_{2,j}}_{2,j}, \ldots, \sigma^{r_{k,j}}_{k,j}$

Second stage

$P \Rightarrow V$: Perform n independent copies of commitments of secrets

$V \Rightarrow P$: Decommit to σ and to $\{\sigma^{1-r_{i,j}}_{i,j}\}^k_{i,j=1}$

$P \Rightarrow V$: Answer according to the value of σ if $\sigma^0_{i,j} \oplus \sigma^1_{i,j} = \sigma$ is satisfied

consists of two stages, which is illustrated in Table 2.5. In the first stage, the verifier will commit to a random n-bit string σ and to two sequences $\{\sigma^0_{i,j}\}^k_{i,j=1}$ and $\{\sigma^1_{i,j}\}^k_{i,j=1}$. Each of the sequences consists of k^2 random n-bit strings, such that for every i,j the value of $\sigma^0_{i,j} \oplus \sigma^1_{i,j} = \sigma$. The total number of committed strings in this step is $2 \cdot k^2 + 1$. This is followed by k iterations between the prover and the verifier. In the jth iteration, the prover will send a random k-bit string, $r_j = r_{1,j}, r_{2,j}, \ldots, r_{k,j}$, and the verifier will decommit k strings of $\sigma^{r_{1,j}}_{1,j}, \sigma^{r_{2,j}}_{2,j}, \ldots, \sigma^{r_{k,j}}_{k,j}$. After first stage, the verifier has opened a total of k^2 strings in the two sequences.

In the second stage, the prover and the verifier will engage in a three-round protocol. After the prover commits secret values about the statement to the verifier, the challenge question σ will be decommitted with all the σ, $\{\sigma^{1-r_{i,j}}_{i,j}\}^k_{i,j=1}$ that were not revealed in the first stage. Upon checking that the strings satisfy the constraint ($\sigma^0_{i,j} \oplus \sigma^1_{i,j} = \sigma$), the prover decommits the corresponding value to the verifier.

Both the RK and the PRS protocols follow the same structure of adding a preamble phase to the basic protocol. This phase is only used for successful simulation to prove the zero-knowledge property. Applying this protocol, Blum's Hamiltonian cycle concurrent ZKP has been demonstrated. Thus, every language in NP has a concurrent ZKP system. A concurrent ZKP for the 0–1 simple knapsack of Table 2.6 that is shown in Section 4.9 yields the PRS protocol in Table 2.7.

A detailed description is given as follows: In the first stage, the verifier will commit an n-bit random string σ and $2k^2$ n'-bit random strings as shown in Table 2.8 with the restriction that $\sigma^0_{i,j} \oplus \sigma^1_{i,j} = \sigma$ as shown in Table 2.9.

Table 2.6 Basic ZKP for 0–1 Simple Knapsack

Common input: n items, each item i with weight w_i and a weight constraint W.

P1: The prover prepares all the black boxes.

V1: Upon receiving $(2 \cdot n + m \cdot n + 2 \cdot C_2^m)$ black boxes, the verifier has two choices:

$\alpha = 0$: The verifier asks the prover to open all the boxes to verify if they satisfy the original simple knapsack problem.

$\alpha = 1$: The verifier asks the prover to open a subset of the summation boxes S_i with $\sum S_i = W$. The verifier also asks to open all the pairs of boxes to check if $Result = 0$ within the subset of S_i.

P2: The prover opens the appropriate boxes according to the two random requests from the verifier (either all the boxes describing the knapsack problem or whose boxes where W is equal to some summation S_i with unique item).

V2: The verifier accepts the proof if the prover complies and rejects otherwise.

For the next $2k$ iterations, the verifier will decommit k strings in each iteration to the prover as shown in Table 2.10:

In the second stage, the prover will make independent copies of $P1$ in Table 2.6 with n' parallel verifiers. The verifier will decommit the σ and remaining $k^2 \; \sigma_{i,j}^{1-r_{i,j}}$ to the prover. The prover will execute n' copies of $P2$ in Table 2.6 if the k^2 strings in the first stage and k^2 strings in the second stage satisfy $\sigma_{i,j}^0 \oplus \sigma_{i,j}^1 = \sigma$. The verifier will accept only if all the conditions are satisfied.

In the actual execution of the protocol, since the prover does not know the value of σ, the protocol would be a proof system for 0–1 simple knapsack with soundness error $1/2^{n'}$. The sole purpose of the first stage is to allow the simulator to know the value of σ. As long as the simulator makes the verifier reveal both $\sigma_{i,j}^0$ and $\sigma_{i,j}^1$ for some i, j, it can simulate the rest of the protocol by adjusting the $P1$ in Table 2.6 according to the value of $\sigma = \sigma_{i,j}^0 \oplus \sigma_{i,j}^1$.

5.2 Efficiency Considerations

Round complexity is considered as a very important complexity measure for cryptographic protocols. It indicates the number of message exchanges taking place in the protocol. Typically, a constant number of rounds will be a desirable result. Under the assumptions of the existence of one-way functions, ZKPs can be constructed in constant number of rounds by Feigh and Shamir [26], Brassard et al. [37], and Goldreich and Kahan [7,21].

Table 2.7 PRS Concurrent ZKP for 0–1 Simple Knapsack

Common input: n items, each item i with weight w_i and a weight constraint W. A parameter k is used for determining the number of rounds and also works as the security parameter that represents the number of concurrent executions.
First stage: $2k + 2$ rounds interactions between the prover and the verifier (independent of the knapsack problem).

Verifier's preliminary step: The verifier selects and commits to an n'-bit string σ and two sequences of n'-bit strings: $\{\sigma_{i,j}^0\}_{i,j=1}^k$, $\{\sigma_{i,j}^1\}_{i,j=1}^k$, for each i, j, $\sigma_{i,j}^0 \oplus \sigma_{i,j}^1 = \sigma$. The total committed strings are $2k^2 + 1$.
For $j = 1, 2, \ldots, k$:
Prover's jth step: Send k-bit string $r_j = r_{1,j}, r_{2,j}, \ldots, r_{k,j}$ to the verifier
Verifier's jth step: Decommit k strings of $\sigma_{1,j}^{r_{1,j}}, \sigma_{2,j}^{r_{2,j}}, \ldots, \sigma_{k,j}^{r_{k,j}}$

Second stage: The prover and the verifier engage in n' parallel executions of Basic ZKP for the 0–1 simple knapsack.
$\hat{P}1$: The prover will prepare boxes for n' parallel independent executions, which means there will be $n' \cdot (2 \cdot n + m \cdot n + 2 \cdot C_2^m)$ black boxes. Each set of $(2 \cdot n + m \cdot n + 2 \cdot C_2^m)$ black boxes is generated independently and contains the different commitment of the same knapsack problem.
$\hat{V}1$: The verifiers decommit to σ and remaining $\{\sigma_{i,j}^{1-r_{i,j}}\}_{i,j=1}^k$, which are not revealed in the first stage.
$\hat{P}2$: The prover checks that the verifier has properly decommitted to the value by checking $\sigma_{i,j}^0 \oplus \sigma_{i,j}^1 = \sigma$. Each bit in σ is the question from the verifier for each execution. If so, the prover opens the appropriate boxes according to each bit value of σ for each execution (either all the boxes within one set which describes the knapsack problem correctly or under one set W is equal some summation of S_i with unique item).
$\hat{V}2$: The verifier conducts the verification of the prover's proofs based on the result of $\hat{P}2$.

Table 2.8 $2k^2$ Randomly Generated Strings

$\sigma_{1,1}^0$	$\sigma_{1,2}^0$	$\ldots$	$\sigma_{1,k}^0$	$\sigma_{1,1}^1$	$\sigma_{1,2}^1$	$\ldots$	$\sigma_{1,k}^1$
$\sigma_{2,1}^0$	$\sigma_{2,2}^0$	$\ldots$	$\sigma_{2,k}^0$	$\sigma_{2,1}^1$	$\sigma_{2,2}^1$	$\ldots$	$\sigma_{2,k}^1$
$\ldots$	$\ldots$	$\ldots$	$\ldots$	$\ldots$	$\ldots$	$\ldots$	$\ldots$
$\sigma_{k,1}^0$	$\sigma_{k,2}^0$	$\ldots$	$\sigma_{k,k}^0$	$\sigma_{k,1}^1$	$\sigma_{k,2}^1$	$\ldots$	$\sigma_{k,k}^1$

Table 2.9 Constraints on Strings

$\sigma_{1,1}^0 \oplus \sigma_{1,1}^1 = \sigma$	$\sigma_{1,2}^0 \oplus \sigma_{1,2}^1 = \sigma$	$\ldots$	$\sigma_{1,k}^0 \oplus \sigma_{1,k}^1 = \sigma$
$\sigma_{2,1}^0 \oplus \sigma_{2,1}^1 = \sigma$	$\sigma_{2,1}^0 \oplus \sigma_{2,2}^1 = \sigma$	$\ldots$	$\sigma_{2,k}^0 \oplus \sigma_{2,k}^1 = \sigma$
$\ldots$	$\ldots$	$\ldots$	$\ldots$
$\sigma_{k,1}^0 \oplus \sigma_{k,1}^1 = \sigma$	$\sigma_{k,2}^0 \oplus \sigma_{k,2}^1 = \sigma$	$\ldots$	$\sigma_{k,k}^0 \oplus \sigma_{k,k}^1 = \sigma$

Table 2.10 Preamble Messages

$(P1)$: The prover will send a random k-bit string $r_1 = r_{1,1}, r_{2,1}, \ldots, r_{k,1}$
$(V1)$: The verifier will decommit $\sigma_{1,1}^{r_{1,1}}, \sigma_{2,1}^{r_{2,1}}, \ldots, \sigma_{k,1}^{r_{k,1}}$
$(P2)$: The prover will send a random k-bit string $r_2 = r_{1,2}, r_{2,2}, \ldots, r_{k,2}$
$(V2)$: The verifier will decommit $\sigma_{1,2}^{r_{1,2}}, \sigma_{2,2}^{r_{2,2}}, \ldots, \sigma_{k,2}^{r_{k,2}}$
$(\ldots)$
(Pk): The prover will send a random k-bit string $r_k = r_{1,k}, r_{2,k}, \ldots, r_{k,k}$
(Vk): The verifier will decommit $\sigma_{1,k}^{r_{1,k}}, \sigma_{2,k}^{r_{2,k}}, \ldots, \sigma_{k,k}^{r_{k,k}}$

In Ref. [21], Goldreich and Kahan presented how to reduce the error probability of interactive proofs that have constant error probability without increasing the round complexity and while preserving their zero-knowledge property. They are SZKPs whose soundness condition requires that nobody, even with unbounded computational ability, can fool the verifier into accepting the false statements except with negligible probability.

Recall that commitment schemes are commonly used to construct ZKPs with two phases. The first phase is called commit. The verifier will not know which value it is if the prover commits a value. The second phase is called reveal. The prover will send some auxiliary information that allows the verifier to reveal the uniquely committed value in order to assure that it is the original value. Two properties named secrecy and nonambiguity are involved [21]:

- Secrecy: At the end of the commit phase, the verifier does not gain any information of the prover's value.
- Nonambinguity: In the reveal phase, with the transcript of the interaction in the commit phase, there exists only one value that the verifier may accept as a legal reveal of the commitment.

Two different commitment schemes have been presented to construct constant-round ZKPs [21]:

- Standard commitment scheme: The nonambiguity requirement is absolute (makes no reference to the computational power of the adversary), whereas the secrecy requirement is computational (refers only to probabilistic polynomial-time adversaries).
- Perfect commitment schemes: The secrecy requirement is absolute, while the nonambiguity requirement is computational.

Goldreich and Kahan presented how to construct constant-round ZKPs for every set in NP, assuming the strong intractability assumptions (the existence of claw-free collections). The claw-free collection implies the existence of one-way functions, but the converse might not be true. Generally, four steps are involved in constructing a round-efficient ZKP [21]:

1. The verifier commits to a challenge. This is usually implemented by two rounds/messages.
2. The prover commits to a sequence of values.
3. The verifier decommits either properly or not.
4. Depending on the verifier's proper decommitment, the prover decommits to the corresponding values.

Based on this construction of constant-round ZKP for NP, Goldreich proved that security will be preserved in the two extreme schedulings of concurrent executions [33]: one is the case of parallel execution, and the other is of concurrent execution under the timing model. The black-box simulator technique is used for zero-knowledge property verification.

5.3 Knowledge Complexity

Knowledge complexity is introduced by Goldwasser *et al.* [5] to measure the computational advantage obtained by interaction. Anything obtained during the interaction will be considered as knowledge. How to quantify the amount of knowledge obtained by interaction is more challenging. One definitional approach is trying to bound the amount of knowledge by the number of bits that are communicated in an alternative interaction that allows to simulate the original interaction. To be more concrete, one party is said to yield at most $k(|x|)$ bits of knowledge if the variation distance between interactive proof system denoted as $(P, V)(x)$ and a simulator denoted as is bounded above by $1 - 2^{-k(|x|)} + |x|^{-c}$. x is the input string. $k(|x|) = \frac{\log(|x|)}{O(1)}$ [38].

5.4 Noninteractive Zero Knowledge

The noninteractive ZKP system was defined by Blum, Feldman, and Micali. It consists of three entities: a prover, a verifier, and a uniformly selected reference string. The reference string is not selected by either parties, but is selected by a trusted third party [21]. The reference string is public to the prover as well as the verifier. The interaction between the two parties is only a single message sent from the prover to the verifier. Then, it is left for the verifier to reach the final decision.

Noninteractive ZKP systems have many applications such as the construction of public-key encryption and signature schemes. What is more, ZKP can be derived by combining a secure coin-flipping protocol with a noninteractive ZKP system [21]. Thus, the round complexity of this ZKP depends on the round complexity of the coin-flipping protocol and on whether it can be securely performed in parallel many times.

6. CONCLUSION

This chapter presented a survey on ZKPs with backgrounds, important concepts, existing applications for NP problems, composition operations, and efficiency considerations. It constructed ZKPs for two NP problems: exact cover and 0–1 simple knapsack based on Blum's protocol for Hamiltonicity. Applying the PRS protocol, a concurrent ZKP for 0–1 simple knapsack is provided and explained in detail.

The notion of zero knowledge originated with the efforts to formalize problems during the design of cryptographic protocols. ZKPs have been shown in many applications of the cryptographic area such as identity verification, authentication, key exchange, and enforcing the honest behavior while maintaining privacy. In an authentication system, one party wants to prove its identity to a second party via some secret information but does not want the second party to learn anything about this secret. One of the classic authentications based on ZKPs is the Feige–Fiat–Shamir proof of identity [16].

The discovery of ZKPs for all of NP has played an important role in secure computation where several parties engage in a protocol to jointly compute a function on their private inputs in a way that no party learns anything other than the output of the protocol. Since ZKPs can be viewed as a special case of secure two-party computation, every party can use ZKPs to convince each other that it is following the specific protocol without revealing its private input. This application was first developed by Goldreich, Micali, and Wigderson in Ref. [6]. A general construction of a ZKP for an NP relation, which makes a black-box use of a secure protocol for a related multiparty functionality, was presented in Ref. [39].

ZKP can also be a good solution to some interesting problems. For example, in Ref. [40], the author proposed a new ZKP of identity scheme based on visual cryptography, visual ZKP of identity, that has been built with only Boolean OR operations. In Ref. [41], the author introduced cryptographic and physical ZKP systems for solutions of Sudoku puzzles, which are also known as NP problem.

Existing ZKPs are iterative in nature; their protocols require multiple communication rounds. Most of ZKPs are based on some complexity assumptions (e.g., the existence of one-way function such as quadratic residuosity, factoring, discrete log, etc.). Researchers still try to find a model in which ZKPs for all of NP could be obtained without any assumptions. In secure computation, it is realized that the complexity assumptions could be removed by working in a model with private communication channels.

The further work of ZKPs could go between cryptography and complexity theory. Non-black-box ZKP has begun to inspire complexity theorists to reexamine whether known limitations of black-box reduction can be bypassed with various types of non-black-box reductions. Another direction is to find common variants of ZKPs [17], such as noninteractive zero knowledge, proofs and arguments of knowledge, and witness indistinguishable protocols.

REFERENCES

[1] A. Shamir, How to share a secret, Commun. ACM 22 (1979) 612–613.
[2] A. Juels, M. Sudan, A fuzzy vault scheme, International Symposium of Information Theory, 2002, pp. 408–425.
[3] W. Jiang, C. Clifton, A secure distributed framework for achieving k-anonymity, Special Issue VLDB J. Privacy-Preserving Data Manage. (2006) 180–187.
[4] J. McLean, Security models and information flow, Proceedings of the IEEE Symposium on Research in Security and Privacy, 1990, pp. 180–187.
[5] S. Goldwasser, S. Micali, C. Rackoff, The knowledge complexity of interactive proof system, SIAM J. Comput. 18 (1989) 186–208.
[6] O. Goldreich, S. Micali, A. Wigderson, Proofs that yield nothing but their validity or all languages in NP have zero-knowledge proof systems, J. ACM 38 (3) (1991) 691–729.
[7] O. Goldriech, Zero-knowledge: twenty years after its invention, IACR Cryptology ePrint Archive 2002 (2002): 186.
[8] Zero Knowledge Proof. http://en.wikipedia.org/wiki/Zero_knowledge_proof (Accessed on October 12, 2011).
[9] S. Goldwasser, S. Micali, Probabilistic encryption, J. Comput. Syst. Sci. 28 (2) (1984) 270–299.
[10] A. C. Yao, Theory and application of trapdoor functions, Proceedings of the 23rd Annual Symposium on Foundations of Computer Science, SFCS'82, 1982, pp. 80–91.
[11] B. Barak, How to go beyond the black-box simulation barrier, 42nd IEEE Symposium on Foundations of Computer Science, 2001, pp. 106–115.
[12] G. I. Simari, A primer on zero knowledge protocols, http://cs.uns.edu.ar/~gis/publications/zkp-simari2002.pdf (Accessed on October 12, 2011).
[13] U. Feige, A. Shamir, Witness indistinguishability and witness hiding protocols, 22nd ACM Symposium on the Theory of Computing, 1990, pp. 416–426.
[14] O. Goldreich, H. Krawczyk, On the composition of zero knowledge proof systems, SIAM J. Comput. 25 (1) (1996) 169–192.
[15] L. Babai, Trading group theory for randomness, 17th ACM Symposium on the Theory of Computing, 1985, pp. 421–429.

[16] U. Feige, A. Fiat, A. Shamir, Zero knowledge proof of identity, 19th STOC, 1986, pp. 210–217.

[17] S. Vadhan, The complexity of zero knowledge, Proc. FSTTCS'07: Foundations of Software Technology and Theoretical Computer Science, pp. 52–70, Springer Berlin Heidelberg, 2007.

[18] G. Brassard, C. Crepeau, Zero-knowledge simulation of Boolean circuits, Cypto86, Springer-Verlag Lecture Notes in Computer Science, vol. 263, 1987, pp. 223–233.

[19] G. Jain, Zero knowledge proofs: a survey, Technical Report University of Pennsylvania.

[20] R. M. Karp, Reducibility among combinatorial problems, Complexity of Computer Computations, Proc. Sympos., 1972, pp. 85–103.

[21] O. Goldreich, A. Kahan, How to construct constant-round zero-knowledge proof systems for NP, J. Cryptol. 9 (3) (1996) 167–190.

[22] A. C. Yao, How to generate and exchange secrets, Proceedings of the 27th Annual Symposium on Foundations of Computer Science, IEEE, 1986, pp. 162–167.

[23] C. Tang, Z. Hao, Perfect zero-knowledge argument of knowledge with negligible error probability in two-round for NP from any one-way permutation, in: 2010 International Conference on Communications and Mobile Computing, 2010.

[24] G. Barssard, D. Chaum, C. Crepeau, Minumum disclosure proofs of knowledge, Comput. Syst. Sci. 37 (2) (1988) 156–189.

[25] U. Feigh, D. Lapidot, A. Shamir, Multiple noninteractive zero-knowledge proofs under general assumptions, J. Comput. 29 (1) (1999) 1–28.

[26] U. Feige, A. Shamir, Zero knowledge proof of knowledge in two rounds, Lecture Notes of Computer Science Advances in Cryptology CRYPTO89, vol. 435, 1990, pp. 526–544.

[27] Petersen Graph. http://en.wikipedia.org/wiki/Petersen_graph (Accessed on October 12, 2011).

[28] A. Mohr, A survey of zero knowledge proofs with applications to cryptography, Southern University at Carbondale.

[29] R. Impagliazzo, M. Yung, Direct minimum-knowledge computations, Advances in Cryptology - Crypto'87, Springer Berlin Heidelberg, vol. 293, (1987) 40–51.

[30] R.C. Merkle, S. Member, Ieee, M.E. Hellman, S. Member, Hiding information and signatures in trapdoor knapsacks, IEEE Trans. Inform. Theor. 24 (1978) 525–530.

[31] O. Goldreich, S. Micali, A. Wigderson, How to play any mental game, Proc. 19th Annual ACM symposium on Theory of Computing, ACM, (1987) 218–229.

[32] A. Rosen, O. Goldreich, Concurrent Zero-Knowledge, Springer, 2006.

[33] O. Goldreich, Concurrent zero knowledge with timing, revisited, 34th ACM Symposium on the Theory of Computing, 2002, pp. 332–340.

[34] C. Dwork, M. Naor, A. Sahai, Concurrent zero-knowledge, 30th ACM Symposium on the Theory of Computing, 1998, pp. 409–418.

[35] R. Richardson, J. Kilian, On the concurrent composition of zero-knowledge proofs, Advances in Cryptology-EuroCrypt99, 1999, pp. 415–431, Springer Berlin Heidelberg.

[36] M. Prabhakaran, A. Rosen, A. Sahai, Concurrent zero knowledge with logarithmic round-complexity, in: 43rd FOCS, 2002, pp. 366–375.

[37] G. Brassard, C. Crepeau, M. Yung, Everything in NP can be argued in perfect zero-knowledge in a bounded number of rounds, Lecture Notes in Computer Science Advances in Cryptology EUROCRYPT 89, 1990, pp. 192–195.

[38] O. Goldreich, E. Petrank, Quantifying knowledge complexity, 32nd FOCS, 1995, pp. 59–68.

[39] Y. Ishai, E. Kushilevitz, R. Ostrovsky, A. Sahai, Zero-knowledge from secure multi-party computation, STOC 07, 2007, pp. 21–30.

[40] A. M. Jaafar, A. Samsudin, Visual zero-knowledge proof of identity scheme: a new approach, Computer Research and Development, 2010 Second International Conference on, pp. 205–212, IEEE, 2010.

[41] R. Gradwohl, M. N. B. Pinkas, G. N. Rothblum, Cryptographic and physical zero-knowledge proof systems for solutions for sudoku puzzles, In Fun with Algorithms, pp. 166–182, Springer Berlin Heidelberg, 2007.

[42] M. Blum, How to prove a theorem so no one else can claim it, Proc. Int. Congress Mathematicians 1 (2) (1987) 1444–1451.

ABOUT THE AUTHORS

Li Feng, Ph.D. student, received her BE in 2002 and ME in 2005 at Beijing University of Chemical Technology. Currently, she is in a Ph.D. program in Computer Science at Missouri University of Science and Technology in Rolla, MO, USA. Her research interest is in the area of computer security in distributed embedded systems that involve security protocol analysis and information flow quantification in cross-disciplinary architectures.

Bruce McMillin is currently a Professor of Computer Science and Director of the Center for Information Assurance at Missouri S&T, Rolla, MO, USA. He leads and participates in interdisciplinary teams in formal methods for fault tolerance and security in distributed embedded systems with an eye toward critical infrastructure protection. He is leading the distributed grid intelligence project of the Future Renewables Engineering Research Center.

CHAPTER THREE

Similarity of Private Keyword Search over Encrypted Document Collection

Yousef Elmehdwi, Wei Jiang, Ali Hurson
Department of Computer Science, Missouri S&T, Rolla, Missouri, USA

Contents

Advances in Computers, Volume 94
ISSN 0065-2458
http://dx.doi.org/10.1016/B978-0-12-800161-5.00003-7

Abstract

Due to its cost-efficiency, flexibility, and offload of administrative overhead, cloud computing has become a viable option for organizations to outsource their data and services. To protect data confidentiality, sensitive data need to be encrypted before outsourced to a cloud. In such case, the task of query processing over encrypted data becomes not trivial. A typical example is a private keyword search where a collection of encrypted documents is stored on a cloud and a user retrieves a subset of documents from the collection containing a given set of keywords. In the process, the set of keywords and the original documents are never disclosed to the cloud. To solve this problem, many schemes have been proposed to allow users to securely search over encrypted document collection through exact and similarity keyword matching. In this chapter, we provided a comprehensive literature survey on the existing schemes of private keyword search.

LIST OF ABBREVIATIONS

ASE Asymmetric searchable encryption
LSH Locality sensitive hashing
PKS Private keyword search
SSE Symmetric searchable encryption

1. INTRODUCTION

Cloud computing [1,2] enables an entity to outsource its database and data processing functionalities. The cloud provides access mechanisms for querying and managing the hosted database. On one hand, by outsourcing, the data owner can get the benefits of reduced data management costs, less overhead of data storage, and improved quality of service. On the other hand, since the cloud cannot be fully trusted, preserving data confidentiality and query privacy become an challenging task. To mitigate these security concerns, it is desirable to encrypt sensitive data before outsourced to a cloud [3]. However, data encryption restricts cloud's ability to perform fundamental data processing functionality such as keyword search without disclosing the original data and user queries. In the literature, such a keyword search task over outsourced and encrypted data is commonly termed as Private keyword search (PKS).

The goal of PKS is to retrieve a subset of documents from a document collection that contains a user query (a set of keywords). The document collection, the user query, and the retrieved results are encrypted so that the server who processed this keyword search does not learn any information regarding the original documents and the content of a user's query. A general

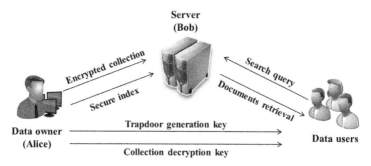

Figure 3.1 Architecture of PKS over outsourced document collection [4].

architecture of PKS is presented in Fig. 3.1 which is a generalization of the schemes in Refs. [3–7]. PKS consists of three main parties: the data owner, the data users, and the server (e.g., cloud). Suppose a data owner Alice has a collection of n sensitive documents $D = \{d_1, \dots, d_n\}$, and she wants to outsource D to a remote server Bob. To ensure data confidentiality, Alice encrypts her D before outsourcing to Bob in such a way that Bob cannot infer any information about D except for what Alice allows to disclose. Let the encrypted document collection denoted by $C = \{c_1, \dots, c_n\}$.

In this setting, authorized users should be able to selectively retrieve the documents from Bob. In order to enable PKS over C, Alice initially creates a secure search index I (formally defined in Section 2.3) over a set of p predefined distinct keywords $W = \{w_1, \dots, w_p\}$ extracted from D. Then, she outsources C along with I to Bob. The secure index I is used as a clue to search over encrypted documents by allowing Bob to test for presence or absence of keywords using a trapdoor function (discussed in Section 2.3) associated with the keywords in a user's search query.

Most existing PKS schemes are constructed based on searchable encryption [8–12] which is a family of cryptographic protocols that facilitate PKS directly on encrypted document collection C. Existing PKS techniques generally utilize two searching criteria: exact and similar. Exact search does not tolerate minor typos and format inconsistencies that happen frequently in typical user queries [13]. However, similar keyword search can deal with misspelled, partial or incomplete keywords in a user query. Since the similarity metrics adopted in PKS can capture exact matches, in this chapter, we use PKS to represent both situations. In addition, some existing PKS schemes differentiate between fuzzy keyword search and similar keyword search. Technically speaking, there is no difference between the two. Thus, to be consist, we will adopt similar keyword search throughout the chapter. The following definition captures the essence of PKS.

Definition 3.1. *Given a collection of n encrypted documents $C = \{c_1, \ldots, c_n\}$ that are characterized by a predefined set of p distinct keywords $W = \{w_1, \ldots, w_p\}$, a query that contains a particular keyword w, and a similarity metric to measure the relevance between the query and the documents. PKS returns a subset of documents whose similarities compared with the given query are greater than a predetermined threshold.*

The goal of this chapter is to provide a comprehensive survey on the existing PKS techniques. The rest of this chapter is organized as follows: Section 2 presents some technical background and security definitions related to PKS, Section 3 discusses the tools used to construct similar keyword set, Section 4 presents different techniques to construct a secure index, Section 5 details the existing PKS schemes, and Section 6 concludes the chapter.

2. BACKGROUND AND DEFINITIONS

To understand the existing PKS schemes, here, we provide an overview on the similarity metric and searchable encryption used to construct the secure index. We will also present the formal definitions and security requirements for PKS in both symmetric and asymmetric settings.

2.1 Similarity Metric

Most PKS schemes adopt edit distance to generate a set of similar terms according to a given keyword. These similar terms will be subsequently used to build the secure index. Edit distance is defined as follows [14]:

Definition 3.2. *The edit distance between two keywords w_i and w_j, $ed(w_i, w_j)$, is the minimum number of edit operations required to transform w_i into w_j. The edit operations under consideration are*

(i) Substitution: changing one character to another in a keyword;
(ii) Deletion: removing one character from a keyword;
(iii) Insertion: adding one character to a keyword.

Example 3.1 *Suppose w_i = "settle" and w_j = "seattle." The edit distance between them is 1, since one edit operation is needed; that is, insertion of "a" between e and t in w_i changes w_i into w_j.*

2.2 Searchable Encryption

Searchable encryption [6,8–11,15] is a basic tool in PKS to construct the secure index and can be categorized into Symmetric searchable encryption (SSE) and Asymmetric searchable encryption (ASE). Most searchable encryption schemes cannot hide data access and search patterns. In addition, they only support exact match in the context of keyword search. As a result, one of the main contributions in the existing PKS schemes is to construct a secure index that support similar keyword search. Detailed survey of existing searchable encryption schemes is provided in Ref. [16]. In this section, we briefly describe the basic structure of searchable encryption in symmetric and asymmetric settings. We emphasize that all the following structures of symmetric and asymmetric encryption schemes are standard definitions and our goal is to highlight the key ideas behind each one.

2.2.1 Symmetric Searchable Encryption

The symmetric searchable encryption (SSE) scheme involves three different entities: data owner, data user, and remote server. In this setting, the data owner encrypts his/her own document collection and uploads the encrypted collection to a remote third-party server so that only the legitimate users, holding the secret key, can retrieve the documents based on a given keyword or a set of keywords. Under SSE, only the data owner can contribute searchable contents, and the data owner and the user share the same secret key. Generally, the definition of any SSE scheme is given as follows [10]:

Definition 3.3. *A symmetric searchable encryption scheme over a document collection $D = \{d_i, \ldots, d_n\}$ has a set of four polynomially bounded algorithms KeyGen, BuildIndex, Trapdoor, and Search:*

- *$k \leftarrow$ **KeyGen**(1^λ): This algorithm is run by a data owner to generate a secret key k according to an input security parameter λ. In addition, it also chooses a pseudo random function $f : \{0,1\}^n \times \{0,1\}^\lambda \leftarrow \{0,1\}^\lambda$ to hide "encrypt" the keywords or build the secure index.*

- *$I \leftarrow$ **BuildIndex**(k, D): This algorithm is run by the data owner to generate a secure index. It takes a secret key k and a data collection D as inputs, and returns a secure index I.*

- *$T_{w_i} \leftarrow$ **Trapdoor**(k, w_i): This algorithm is run by the data user to generate a trapdoor (i.e., a keyed hash value) for a given keyword w_i. It takes a secret key k and a specific keyword $w_i \in W$ as inputs, where W is a keyword set, and outputs a trapdoor $T_{w_i} = f(k, w_i)$.*

- $ID_{w_i} \leftarrow$ **Search(I, T_{w_i}):** *This algorithm is run by the server in order to search for the documents in D that contain a specific keyword w_i. It takes an encrypted index I related to the data collection D and a trapdoor T_{w_i} as input, and outputs ID_{w_i}, a set of document identifiers whose corresponding documents contain the keyword w_i.*

The data owner encrypts the document collection D using a symmetric encryption in conventional manner to generate the encrypted collection C before he/she builds the secure index I.

2.2.2 Asymmetric Searchable Encryption

In ASE scheme, the concept of public key encryption is employed so that every entity can contribute searchable encrypted contents that only the recipient can decrypt. Under this setting, three different entities are involved: a client, a sender, and a remote server. The entity (sender) that generates the data can be different from the one that searches over the data [7,17].

Initially, the client generates a public/private key pair and publishes the public key. With this public key, any sender can generate encrypted contents that only the client can decrypt. Thus, every entity (sender) is able to generate searchable contents without any explicit authorization from the client [18]. Unlike ciphertexts generated from standard public-key encryption schemes, these are searchable upon delegation, meaning that if the data are stored in a remote server, the client can authorize the server to search on his/her behalf by issuing a trapdoor for the target keyword which is generated from his/her private key [19]. Generally, the definition of any ASE scheme is given as follows [11,16,20,21]:

Definition 3.4. *Asymmetric searchable encryption scheme is a collection of four polynomial-time algorithms: KeyGen, BuildIndex, Trapdoor, and Search:*
- $(pk, sk) \leftarrow$ **KeyGen(1^λ):** *this algorithm is run by the client to setup the scheme. It takes a security parameter λ as input and generates his or her public/private key pair (pk, sk). In addition, the client generates the public keyword set W and chooses a pseudo random function $f : \{0,1\}^n \times \{0,1\}^\lambda \leftarrow \{0,1\}^\lambda$. The public key pk is used to store data on a server, and the private key sk is used to retrieve information from that server.*
- $I_{w_i} \leftarrow$ **BuildIndex(pk, w_i):** *This algorithm is run by a sender to produce searchable encryption of w_i. It takes a client's public key pk and a specific keyword $w_i \in W$ as input and outputs an index I_{w_i}.*
- $T_{w_j} \leftarrow$ **Trapdoor(sk, w_j):** *this algorithm is run by the client to generate a trapdoor. It takes client's private key sk and a specific keyword $w_j \in W$ as input and outputs a trapdoor $T_{w_j} = f(sk, w_j)$.*

- $b \leftarrow$ **Search**(pk, I_{w_i}, T_{w_j}): *this algorithm is run by the server to perform search operation. It takes a client's public key pk, an index I_{w_i}, and a trapdoor T_{w_j} as input, and outputs $b = 1$ if $w_i = w_j$, and $b = 0$ otherwise.*

Technically speaking, SSE schemes are based on the symmetric cryptographic primitives such as hash functions and block ciphers [22], whereas ASE schemes built upon the intensive usage of complicated structures such as pairing operations on elliptic curves [23], which are much slower than symmetric cryptographic primitives. Hence, SSE schemes are more efficient than ASE schemes. Such inefficiency disadvantage may limit their practical performance when deployed into a cloud.

2.2.3 Security Requirements

Searchable encryption schemes follow the security definitions defined in Ref. [10]. More specifically, data confidentiality and keyword privacy must be achieved. For efficiency purpose, it is required that nothing should be leaked from the outsourced encrypted document collection and index beyond the search pattern and access patterns of the user queries. The access pattern refers to the outcome of the search result, that is, which documents contain the keyword, whereas the search pattern refers to the possibility of inferring whether two queries were performed for the same keyword and any information derived thereafter from this statement.

Most existing works related to searchable encryption schemes assume the semi-honest adversary model. In the semi-honest model (also referred to as honest-but-curious), the adversary (e.g., cloud) is assumed to follow the prescribed steps of the protocol (i.e., executes all searching operations and returns all search results honestly), but may attempt to learn extra information from the protocol transcript [24,25]. For example, an adversary may try to learn and infer the underlying plaintext information of the encrypted document collection or searchable index.

2.3 Terminologies and Other Basic Tools

In this section, we present the necessary concepts and tools used by the existing PKS schemes discussed in the later part of this chapter.

- **Trapdoors for Keywords:** Trapdoors can be realized by applying a one-way function f on keywords [13]. More formally, it is defined as follows:

  Definition 3.5. *Given a keyword w_i and an index generation secret key sk, the trapdoor of w_i (denoted by T_{w_i}) can be computed as*

  $$T_{w_i} = f(sk, w_i)$$

Given a trapdoor for a keyword, a remote server can perform a search operation over encrypted keywords and recover pointers to the appropriate (encrypted) documents. In other words, the server can test whether the keyword is contained in specific document using the trapdoor of the keyword.

- **Secure Index:** An index is a data structure that stores a document collection to support efficient keyword search. In the literature, there exist two well-known methods to construct indexes: *forward* and *inverted* [16].
  - *Forward index* is an index structure that stores a list of mappings from each document to the corresponding set of keywords that belongs to the document.
  - *Inverted index* is an index structure that stores a list of mappings from each keyword to the corresponding set of document(s) in which the keyword is present [14]. The set of keywords in the index is usually called a dictionary. A document identifier appearing in the list associated with a keyword is called a posting, and the list of document identifiers associated with a given keyword is called a posting list. An example of inverted index is shown in Fig. 3.2B, where w_i denotes ith keyword, and id_i denotes ith document identifier.

A secure index I is constructed over a set of distinct keywords W in a document collection and stored at the server side in order to help the server to perform keyword search. Each keyword is hashed to produce a trapdoor, and I only contains these trapdoor values and their pointers to corresponding documents. Figure 3.2A shows an example of the secure index, where T_{w_i} denotes trapdoor of ith keyword, and id_i denotes ith document identifier. The main intuition behind secure indexing is that users who possess a trapdoor for a keyword $w_i \in W$ can test the index

A

Keywords	Documents identifiers
w_1	id_1, id_3, id_4
w_2	id_2, id_3
w_3	id_2
w_4	id_1

B

Trapdoors	Documents identifiers
T_{w_1}	id_1, id_3, id_4
T_{w_2}	id_2, id_3
T_{w_3}	id_2
T_{w_4}	id_1

Figure 3.2 Examples of inverted and secure indexes. (A) Inverted index. (B) Secure index.

for w_i. Here the trapdoor can only be generated with a secret key known to the users, so the index reveals no information about the original documents to the server [8,10]. From a computational perspective, a secure index allows a remote server to check whether an encrypted document contains a keyword without having to decrypt the entire document [8].

- **Similarity Keyword Set:** Given a collection of n encrypted documents $C = (c_1, \ldots, c_n)$ stored in the cloud server and a set of p distinct keywords $W = \{w_1, \ldots, w_p\}$ with predefined edit distance threshold d, Li *et al.* [4] defined the similarity keyword set based on edit distance as follows:

Definition 3.6. *Given a keyword $w_i \in W$, the similarity keyword set $S_{w_i,d}$ denotes the set of keywords w' that satisfies the property $ed(w_i, w') \leq d$, where $ed(w_i, w')$ is the edit distance between w_i and w'.*

The idea behind similarity keyword set is to build a set consisting of the searched keyword and the nearby words according to the used data representation techniques (e.g., enumeration or wildcard-based techniques, formally defined in Section 3).

- **k-gram:** A k-gram is a contiguous sequence of k characters from a keyword w, where k is a positive integer ranging from 1 to the keyword length [14,26]. In general, the k-gram model can be thought as placing a small window over a keyword, in which only k characters are visible at a time. Given a keyword w, there exist $|w| - k + 1$ k-gram for w, where $|w|$ denotes the length of the keyword w.

Example 3.2 *Given $w = $ "computer" and $k = 2$. Then, the 2-gram set for w, denoted by $Q(w)$, contains seven 2-gram as given below*

$$Q(w) = \{co, om, mp, pu, ut, te, er\}$$

- **Gram Counting Order:** Gram counting order is a transformation function that captures one aspect of the abundant information contained in strings and used to build a B^{ed}-tree index by utilizing k-gram to summarize the string set. It used to design a string order [26], a mapping function that maps each string to an integer value, based on counting the number of k-gram within a string. Specifically, a k-gram set can be represented as a vector in a high dimensional space where each dimension corresponds to a distinct k-gram. To compress the information on the vector space in order to reduce the high storage cost, one can use a hash function to map each-k-gram to a set of L buckets, and count the number of k-gram in each bucket. Hence, the k-gram set can be transformed into a vector of L nonnegative integers [26].

Example 3.3 *Consider a string* $s =$ *"network". For* $k = 2$*, the* k*-gram set for* s *is given by* $Q(s) = \{\$n, ne, et, tw, wo, or, rk, k\$\}$*. Note that the special character "$\$$" is used to denote the beginning or end of a set.*
Figure 3.3 shows a sample process of hashing the eight 2-gram of string s *to four buckets. After the mapping and counting the 2-gram in each bucket, the string* s *is represented by a four-dimensional vector* $v_s = \langle 2, 2, 3, 1 \rangle$ *[26].*

- **Locality Sensitive Hashing:** Locality sensitive hashing (LSH) is an approximation algorithm for near neighbor search in high dimensional spaces [28,29]. The basic idea of LSH is to map (hash) objects using a series of hashing functions into several buckets so as to ensure that, for each function, the probability of collision is much higher for objects which are close to each other than for those which are far apart (similar objects are mapped into the same hash bucket with high probability, while dissimilar ones do not) [3,28]. By doing so, near neighbors can be determined by hashing the query point and retrieving the elements stored in buckets containing that point [29]. LSH uses locality sensitive function families to achieve that. More formally, a LSH is defined as follows [28].

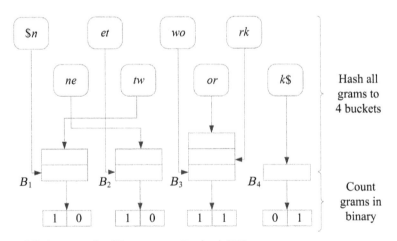

Figure 3.3 An example of 2-gram counting hash [27].

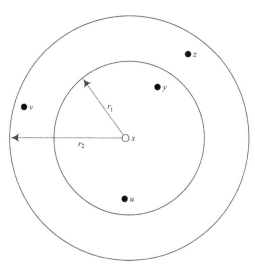

Figure 3.4 LSH example.

Definition 3.7. *Let r_1, r_2 be distances according to the utilized distance metric* $(dist : F \times F \mapsto R)$ *such that $r_1 < r_2$ and p_1, p_2 be probabilities such that* $p_1 > p_2$. *Then, the family of hash functions H is said to be (r_1, r_2, p_1, p_2)-sensitive if for any $x, y \in F$ and $h \in H$, the following properties hold:*

- *if $dist(x, y) \leq r_1$, then $Pr[h(x) = h(y)] \geq p_1$*
- *if $dist(x, y) \geq r_2$, then $Pr[h(x) = h(y)] \leq p_2$*

LSH is useful for similarity search if p_1 is much higher than p_2 for some application specific r_1 and r_2. This is because, search result should contain almost all the items that are close to the query point and it should not contain more than a reasonable amount of dissimilar items [3].

Consider three different points x, y, and z as shown in Fig. 3.4 where $dist(x, y) \leq r_1$ and $dist(x, z) \geq r_2$. The point y, with high probability, will be mapped into the same hash bucket with x whereas z will not.

3. CONSTRUCTING SIMILARITY KEYWORD SET

Given an encrypted document collection $C = (c_1, \ldots, c_n)$, a predefined set of distinct keywords $W = \{w_1, \ldots, w_p\}$, a keyword w' in the searching input with a specified edit distance d, the execution of a PKS protocol should return a set of document identifiers (denoted by $\{ID_{w_i}\}$ whose corresponding documents possibly contain the keyword w_i such that $ed(w_i, w') \leq d$, where $ed(w_i, w')$ defines the edit distance between w_i and w'.

The idea behind PKS is twofold: (1) building up similarity keyword sets that incorporate not only the exact keywords but also the ones that differ slightly due to minor typos and format inconsistencies, and (2) designing an efficient and secure searching approach for document retrieval based on the resulted similarity keyword sets. In this section, we focus on the first part, and we describe two different techniques for constructing the similarity keyword set $S_{w_i,d}$ using edit distance, whereas in Section 5, we focus on the second part.

3.1 Enumeration Technique

Assume that we want to construct the similarity keyword set $S_{w_i,d}$ for each keyword $w_i \in W$ within edit distance d. One way to construct $S_{w_i,d}$ is to enumerate all possible keywords w' that satisfy the similarity criteria $ed(w_i, w') \leq d$. That is, all the keywords within edit distance d from keyword w_i are listed.

Example 3.4 *Given the keyword $w_i =$ "search" and the predefined edit distance $d = 1$. The following set contains similar keywords generated after a substitution operation on the first character of w_i.*

$$S_{search,1} = \{aearch, bearch, \ldots, yearch, zearch\}$$

Recall from Definition 3.2 that substitution, deletion, and insertion are the three kinds of operations used in computing the edit distance. Since the number of candidate (possible) words satisfying the similarity criteria $ed(w_i, w') \leq d$ with $d = 1$ and $w_i =$ "search" for deletions is l, and the number of candidate words for substitutions and insertions is $(l \times 26) - l$ and $(l+1) \times 26$, respectively, where l denotes the size of keyword w_i. Furthermore, in case $ed(w_i, w') = 0$, the original keyword w_i will be considered as one possible outcome in the resulted similarity keyword set which adds up to the total number. Hence, the total number of all similar words on $w_i =$ "search" constructed in this way is $(2 * l + 1) \times 26 + 1 = 13 \times 26 + 1$, where $l = |w_i| = 6$.

3.2 Wildcard-Based Technique

This technique is an efficient and practical way for constructing similarity keyword set with regard to both storage and search efficiency [4,13]. The wildcard-based technique eliminates the need for enumerating all the similarity keywords; therefore, the size of the resulting similarity keyword set is significantly reduced. The idea here is to consider only the position of the three primitive edit operations. Specifically, a wildcard "*" is used to denote all three operations of character insertion, deletion and substitution at the same position. Wildcard-based similarity keyword set can be defined as follows [4,13,30]:

Definition 3.8. *The wildcard-based similarity keyword set of w_i with edit distance d is denoted as $S_{w_i,d} = \{S'_{w_i,0}, S'_{w_i,1}, \ldots, S'_{w_i,d}\}$, where $S'_{w_i,j}$ denotes the set of words w' with j wildcards and $0 \leq j \leq d$. Note that each wildcard represents an edit operation on w_i and $S'_{w_i,0}$ denotes the original keyword w_i.*

Example 3.5 *Given the keyword $w_i =$ "search" with a predefined edit distance $d = 1$, the wildcard-based similarity keyword set can be constructed as:*

$$S_{search,1} = \{search, *search, s*earch, s*earch, \ldots, searc*, search*\}$$

Since the deletion and substitution operations occur on the same position, then the number of candidate (possible) words satisfying the similarity criteria $ed(w_i, w') \leq d$ with $d = 1$ for deletion and substitution is only l, and the number of candidate words for insertions is $l + 1$. Furthermore, $S'_{w_i,0}$ will contribute 1 to the total number, since it represents the original keyword w_i. Hence, the total number of all similar words on $w_i =$ "search" constructed in this way is $2 * l + 1 + 1 = 13 + 1$, where $l = |w_i| = 6$.

From the above discussion, it should be clear that the size of $S'_{w_i,d}$ obtaining in the wildcard-based technique is $O(l^d)$ whereas $O(l^d \times 26^d)$ in the enumeration-based technique. Technically speaking, for a given keyword w_i with length l and an edit distance $d = 1$, the size of similarity keyword set $S_{w_i,1}$ will be only $2 * l + 1 + 1$ opposing to $(2 * l + 1) \times 26 + 1$ obtained in the enumeration technique. Hence, the larger the value of edit distance d is, the more storage overhead can be saved using wildcard-based technique [4,30].

4. CONSTRUCTING SECURE INDEX

The index-based technique is a common data structure used as a building block for PKS schemes. Recall that a secure index is a data structure that stores document collections while support efficient PKS over encrypted document collection C. That is, given a trapdoor of a keyword, the index returns a pointer to the encrypted documents that contain the keyword. More specifically, every document $d_i \in D$ will be characterized by a list of keywords which are then used to build a search index I for the document collection. In secure index, the search operation for a keyword can only be performed by users that possess a trapdoor for the keyword where the trapdoor can only be generated with a secret key. In this section, we discuss in more details four different techniques for constructing the secure index over encrypted document collection.

4.1 Inverted-Index-Based Secure Index

Consider a data owner Alice who owns a collection of n documents $D = \{d_1, \ldots, d_n\}$, where each document $d_i \in D$ has a unique identifier id_i, and a set of p distinct keyword $W = \{w_1, \ldots, w_p\}$. An inverted-index-based secure index for the keyword set W can be constructed as follows [4]: Alice extracts first a similarity keyword set $S_{w_i,d}$ for each keyword $w_i \in W$ with a desirable edit distance d using a data representation techniques such as wildcard-based technique (formally defined in Section 3.2). Next, she computes a trapdoors set $\{T_{w_i'}\}$, where $T_{w_i'} = f(\text{sk}, w_i')$, for each $w_i' \in S_{w_i,d}$ with a secret key sk, and then encrypts a set of documents identifiers ID_{w_i} as $\text{Enc}(\text{sk}, ID_{w_i} \parallel w_i)$. Finally, the inverted-index-based secure index I is given as: $\{(\{T_{w_i'}\}_{w_i' \in S_{w_i,d}}, \text{Enc}(\text{sk}, ID_{w_i} \parallel w_i))\}_{w_i \in W}$.

4.2 Symbol-Trie-Based Secure Index

A trie, or prefix tree, is a tree data structure for storing strings (keywords) in sorted order [31]. A symbol-trie-based secure index is a multiway tree constructed by the data owner Alice for storing all the similarity keyword elements of $\{S_{w_i,d}\}_{w_i \in W}$ over a finite symbol set [13,30,32]. The key idea behind this construction is that all trapdoors sharing a common prefix may have common a node. The root is associated with an empty set and the symbols in a trapdoor can be recovered through a search from the root to the leaf that ends the trapdoor [13,30,32].

We summarize the symbol-trie-based secure index I construction as follows [13]: assume $\Delta = \{\alpha_i\}$ is a predefined symbol set, where the number of different symbols is $|\Delta| = 2^\beta$ and each symbol $\alpha_i \in \Delta$ can be denoted by β bits. To build symbol-trie secure index I, Alice computes first $T_{w_i'} = f(\text{sk}, w_i')$ for each $w_i' \in \{S_{w_i,d}\}_{1 \leq i \leq p}$. Then, she divides the hash value into a sequence of symbols as $\alpha_{i_1}, \ldots, \alpha_{i_{s/\beta}}$, where s is the output length of one-way function $f(.)$.

Next, Alice builds a trie I covering all the similarity keywords $w_i \in W$ based on symbols in Δ. Specifically, for each trapdoor sequence, the first symbol is matched with the child of the root of I. If there is existing node equal to the symbol, set it as the current node. Otherwise, the first symbol is added into the trie as the child of the root, and set it as the current node.

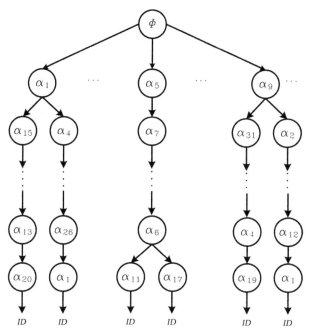

Figure 3.5 An example of symbol-trie-based secure index [13].

Subsequently, the second symbol is matched with the child of the current node. The process is carried out recursively. When the last symbol in each trapdoor is performed, she attaches the corresponding encrypted identifiers $\text{Enc}(\text{sk}, ID_{w_i} || w_i)_{1 \le i \le p}$ as a leaf node into I. Figure 3.5 shows an example of symbol-trie-based secure index I. The paths of trapdoors for different keywords are integrated by merging all the paths with the same prefix into a single tree to support more efficient search.

4.3 LSH-Based Secure Index

The key idea of this construction is based on the property of LSH (formally defined in Section 2.3). Recall that LSH maps objects into several buckets such that similar objects have much higher probability to hash to the same buckets (collide in some buckets) than dissimilar ones. We summarize the LSH-based secure index I construction as follows [3]: consider a data owner Alice who owns a collection of n documents $D = \{d_1, \ldots, d_n\}$. Alice extracts a set of keywords of each document in a collection D. Let d_i be the ith document and $W_i = \{w_{i_1}, \ldots, w_{i_z}\}$ be the set of keywords that characterizes d_i. To apply LSH, it might be required to translate the extracted keywords to vectors in some metric space in case the utilized similarity metric does not have locality sensitive function family. For example, let the keywords are strings and the similarity metric is edit distance. In such case, there is no known locality sensitive function family for the edit distance. Therefore, the strings can be translated into the Euclidean space by approximately preserving the relative edit distance between them [33] in order to use any available families that are defined for the Euclidean distance. Alice maps keywords into a vector set such that $\vec{W}_i = \rho(W_i)$ where $\vec{W}_i = \{\vec{w}_{i_1}, \ldots, \vec{w}_{i_z}\}$.

Assume that there is a locality sensitive function family functions H available for the utilized similarity metric. Alice first constructs a locality sensitive function $g : (g_1, \ldots, g_\lambda)$ from H. Next, Alice maps/hashes each keyword vectors $\vec{w}_{i_j} \in \vec{W}_i$, where $1 \leq j \leq z$ to λ buckets via composite hash functions $g_1, \ldots, g_\lambda$. Thus, each keyword vector is mapped into λ buckets via g. Let V_{B_k} denote a bucket vector of length n bits (here B_k is the bucket identifier), where ith bit corresponds to ith document. Note that the bucket vector is initializing as a zero vector of size n. The ith bit of a bucket vector ($V_{B_k}[id_l]$) is set to 1, where id_l denotes the identifier of document d_l, if at least one of the keywords of the corresponding document is hashed to that bucket. Each bucket vector represents the set of document collection whose keywords are hashed to that bucket. Figure 3.6 shows an example of the buckets construction for a specific keyword vector (says $\vec{w}_{i_j}$).

Finally, all bucket identifiers and contents are encrypted using two secret keys K_{id}, K_{payloads}. Let B_k be a kth bucket identifier, V_{B_k} be the

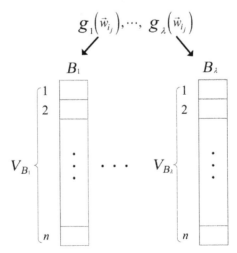

Figure 3.6 An example of buckets construction for a keyword vector $\vec{w}_{i_j}$.

bit vector for B_k, then $[\pi_{B_k}, \sigma_{V_{B_k}}] \in I$, where $\pi_{B_k} \leftarrow \mathrm{Enc}_{K_{id}}(B_k)$, $\sigma_{V_{B_k}} \leftarrow \mathrm{Enc}_{K_{\text{payload}}}(V_{B_k})$.

4.4 B^{ed}-Tree-Based Secure Index

B^{ed}-tree is a B^+-tree-based secure index with the benefit of supporting similarity searches and joins queries on edit distance and normalized edit distance [26,34]. As given in Refs. [26,27], B^{ed}-tree-based secure index I can be constructed based on gram counting order (formally defined in Section 2.3) on the top of B^+-tree. Specifically, a data owner Alice first generates similarity keyword sets $S_{w_i,j}$ with edit distances $j = 1, \ldots, d$ for each $w_i \in W$. Then, for each $S_{w_i,j}$ with edit distance j, she generates a bloom filter $bf_{w_{i,j}}$ based on the words in the associated keyword set. Next, she computes the hash value h_{w_i} of a keyword w_i, constructs the data vector v_{w_i} based on gram counter order and encrypts the list of document identifiers that contain a keyword w_i, $\mathrm{Enc}(sk, ID_{w_i}||w_i)$. Finally, she inserts a leaf node containing the following data structure into the index I: $[v_{w_i}, h_{w_i}, \{bf_{w_{i,1}}, \ldots, bf_{w_{i,d}}\}, \{\mathrm{Enc}(sk, ID_{w_i}||w_i)\}]$. Typical B^+ index tree technique as described in Ref. [26] is used to insert leaf nodes.

4.5 Bilinear-Based Secure Index

Bilinear-based secure index is an index built by the cloud server over encrypted collection in a secure way. That is, the cloud constructs the index based on bilinear pairing [35] without knowing the encrypted keywords. We summarize the bilinear-based secure index I construction as follows [36]: the cloud publishes the bilinear pairing parameters $\mathrm{param} = (p, G_1, G_2, e, g)$, where G_1 and G_2 are two cyclic multiplication group of prime order p and g; $e : G_1 \times G_1 \rightarrow G_2$ be a bilinear map between them.

For simplicity, we consider a sender has a document d_i with identifier id_i and a set of z keywords $W_i = \{w_{i_1}, \ldots, w_{i_z}\}$. Upon receiving param and the client's public key pk, the sender generates a random number $r \in Z_p^*$ and computes $s_{a_j} = g^r$ and $s_{b_j} = w_{i_j}^r$ for each $w_{i_j} \in W_i$. Next, he/she runs the keyword encryption algorithm *IPEFKS* [36] to encrypt each $w_{i_j} \in W_i$, then he/she sends a request contains $\{s_{a_j}, s_{b_j}, IPEFKS(\text{pk}, w_{i_j})\}_{1 \leq j \leq z}$ along with the document identifier id_i and the encrypted document d_i to the cloud.

Assume that there exists a bilinear-based secure index I with m entries at the cloud. That is $\{c_{a_l} = g^{r_l}, c_{b_l} = w_l^{r_l}, IPEFKS(\text{pkpk}, w_l), ID_l\}_{1 \leq l \leq m} \in I$, where ID_l is the set of document identifiers that contain the keyword w_l. Upon receiving the request from the sender, the cloud decides if the keyword w_{i_j} is equal to one of the m keywords in I by using the bilinear property. Specifically, the cloud checks whether the equation $e(s_{a_j}, c_{b_l}) = e(c_{a_l}, s_{b_j})$ holds for a certain $l \in m$. If yes, the cloud adds the document identifier id_i to the set ID_l. Otherwise, the cloud inserts $\{c_{a_{m+1}} = s_{a_j}, c_{b_{m+1}} = s_{b_j}, IPEFKS(\text{pk}, w_{i_j}), ID_{m+1} = id_i\}$ as a new entry to the end of the index I.

5. OVERVIEW OF SOME EXISTING SCHEMES

In this section, we touch upon the details of some basic methods for achieving PKS over encrypted document collection in cloud computing environment.

5.1 Symmetric-Key PKS

Although PKS schemes (e.g., [8–12,15]) allow a user to securely search over encrypted document collection C through keywords and selectively retrieve documents of interest, these techniques are limited to performing an exact search. That is, they cannot carry out a similarity search. Thus, such schemes are not able to support the typographical errors that exist frequently in real-world applications.

To handle such a problem, Li et al. [4] proposed the first symmetric-key PKS scheme that tolerates both minor typos and format inconsistencies in the user searching inputs over encrypted document collection in cloud. They introduced a pioneer and initial attempt on the idea of similarity keyword set (formally defined in Section 2.3). Recall that the similarity should here be understood as minor typos introduced by users when entering the request through their keyboard [37]. The idea behind these similarity keyword sets is to index, before the search phase, not only the exact keywords but also the ones differing slightly according to a fixed bound on the tolerated edit distance d.

The key idea of Li et al. [4] is to enumerate all the similarity keywords that are within a predefined edit distance d to a given keyword. For indexing the resulting similarity variants, they use a secure index. This scheme transforms a single similarity keyword search operation into several exact keyword search operations [36]. Specifically, consider a data owner Alice who owns a collection of n documents $D = \{d_1, \ldots, d_n\}$, where each document $d_i \in D$ has a unique identifier id_i, and a set of p distinct keyword $W = \{w_1, \ldots, w_p\}$. Alice constructs an inverted-index-based secure index

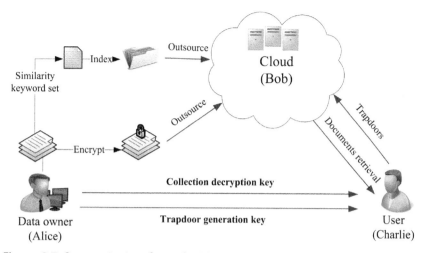

Figure 3.7 Communication flow of PKS over encrypted document collection in cloud [4].

I (discussed in Section 4.1) and outsources it along with the encrypted form of collection C to cloud owned by Bob.

To search the collection for a given keyword w with edit distance k, where $k \leq d$, an authorized user Charlie constructs first a similarity keyword set $S_{w,k}$ for the search keyword w using the same technique used by the data owner Alice for achieving similarity keyword search. Next, he computes the trapdoor set $\{T_{w'}\}_{w' \in S_{w,k}}$ and sends it to Bob. Upon receiving the search request T_w, Bob compares it with the secure index I and returns all the possible encrypted documents identifiers $\{\mathrm{Enc}(\mathrm{sk}, ID_{w_i} \parallel w_i)\}$, where ID_{w_i} denotes a set of documents' identifiers whose corresponding documents contain the keyword w_i. Finally, Charlie decrypts the returned results and retrieves relevant documents of interest. Figure 3.7 shows the communication flow of the proposed PKS scheme.

The succeeding works done by Li *et al.* [13] and Wang *et al.* [30] focus on efficiency. Both authors proposed PKS scheme with symbol–trie-based secure index (discussed in Section 4.2) in order to achieve high efficiency. Similar to Li *et al.* [4], they utilized the wildcard-based technique (formally defined in Section 3) to generate a storage-efficient similarity keyword set $S_{w,d}$ for the keyword w with a desirable edit distance d.

In Ref. [13], Alice constructs a symbol–trie-based secure index I in the same way as that discussed in Section 4.2 and outsources the secure index I along with the encrypted document collection C to cloud owned by Bob. For searching documents containing a keyword w with edit distance

k, where $k \leq d$, Charlie generates $S_{w,k}$ from the keyword w using the same technique used by Alice for achieving similarity keyword search and derives the trapdoor set $\{T_{w'}\}_{w' \in S_{w,k}}$ using a one-way function $f(\text{sk}, .)$, where sk is a secret key, and sends them to Bob. Upon receiving a set of trapdoors as the search request, $\{T_w\}$, Bob divides each entry in the trapdoors set into a sequence of symbols from Δ, performs search over I. Specifically, for each trapdoor sequence, the first symbol is matched with the child of the root of I. If there is existing node equal to the symbol, set it as the current node [38]. Subsequently, the second symbol is matched with the child of the current node. This process is carried and when the current node is the leaf node, Bob returns a set $\{\text{Enc}(\text{sk}, ID_{w_i} || w_i)\}$ attached with this node to Charlie.

However, Wang et al. [30] scheme is slightly different than Li et al. [13] scheme. In Ref. [30], Alice picks two random keys x and y and computes $T'_w = f(x, w'_i)$ as symbols from Δ for each $w'_i \in S_{w_i, i}$ ($1 \leq i \leq p$). She builds up a symbol-trie-based secure index I that covers all the similarity keywords of $w_i \in W$ and attaches $\{\text{Enc}(\text{sk}_{w'_i}, ID_{w_i} || w_i)\}$ for $i = 1, \ldots, p$ to I, where $\text{sk}_{w'_i} = g(y, w'_i)$ and $g(key, .)$ is a pseudo-random function. Then, she outsources these information to Bob. To search for input w with edit distance d, Charlie generates $S_{w,d}$ from his input w and computes trapdoors $T_{w'} = (f(x, w'), g(y, w'))$ for all $w' \in S_{w_i, d}$. Next, he sends a set of trapdoors $\{T_{w'}\}_{w' \in S_{w,d}}$ as a search request to Bob. In fact, the edit distance of user's may be different from the predefined one. Upon receiving the search request, Bob divides each $f(x, w')$ in the trapdoors set into a sequence of symbols from Δ, performs search for each trapdoor over secure index I. Specifically, for each trapdoor sequence, the first symbol is matched with the child of the root of I. If there is existing node equal to the symbol, set it as the current node. Subsequently, the second symbol is matched with the child of the current node. This process is carried and when the current node is the leaf node, Bob uses the corresponding $g(y, w')$ to decrypt the matched entry. Then, he returns a set ID_{w_i} where $ed(w, w_i) \leq d$ to Charlie.

5.2 Verifiable Symmetric-Key PKS

In the literature, most PKS schemes consider only a "honest-but-curious" cloud server adversary model. However, a cloud server, besides its curiosity, may be selfish in order to save its computation ability and/or download bandwidth. Therefore, it is possible that the cloud may execute only a nonzero fraction of the search and return part of the searching result honestly. Motivated by this fact, Chai and Gong [39] first addressed this issue and proposed a verifiable exact PKS scheme, which ensures, apart from protecting data privacy, that the user can verify if cloud has returned incomplete or inaccurate search results. In Ref. [39], the authors consider a computationally bounded adversary model referred to as "semi-honest-but-curious" server model in which the server does not modify the stored documents and the server tries to derive sensitive information from the stored documents, user's search queries as well as search results. Furthermore, the server may forge a fraction of the search outcome and it may execute only a fraction of search operations honestly.

Wang *et al.* [32,38] investigate similar PKS in the scenario of "semi-honest-but-curious" server. They proposed new efficient verifiable similar PKS schemes based on the symbol-trie-based secure index I (discussed in Section 4.2) which do not only support verifiable similar PKS, but also reduce the verifying computation cost and also allows verification of the search outcome.

However, their construction of secure index I is slightly different than in Section 4.2. Specifically, in Ref. [32], a data owner Alice builds a trie I in the same way as shown in Section 4.2 with one difference: each node in the trie contains two attributes (r_0, r_1), where r_0 stores the symbol value; r_1 stores a globally unique value path$||$mem$||F(k, ($path$||$mem$))$, where path contains the sequence of symbols from root to the current node, mem is a bit stream of length 2^β which represents, using bitmap technique, the set of children nodes of the current internal node, and $F(k, .)$ is pseudo-random function with a secret key k. For example, if a current node whose r_0's value is the ith symbol in Δ ($r_0 = \alpha_i$) is a child of the root and has only one child such that it's r_0's value is the jth symbol in Δ (α_j). Then, the jth bit of mem is set to "1," while other bit positions are set to zero. Hence, path $= \alpha_i$, and mem $= \{0 \ldots 010 \ldots 0\}$ [32].

Different from the internal nodes, the identifiers of documents in which the associated keyword appears are stored in r_1 instead of mem. Therefore, in the leaf nodes, $r_1 = $ path$||ID_{w_i}||F(K, ($path$||ID_{w_i}))$ where ID_{w_i} denotes the set for all documents' identifiers whose corresponding documents possibly contain the keyword w_i. Next, Alice attaches $\{ID_{w_i}||g(k, ID_{w_i})\}_{1 \leq i \leq p}$ to I and outsources I with encrypted documents to cloud owned by Bob.

For search input w with edit distance d, Charlie computes the trapdoor $T'_w = f(\text{sk}, w')$ for each $w' \in S_{w,d}$ and sends set of trapdoors $\{T_{w'}\}_{w' \in S_{w,d}}$ to cloud owned by Bob. Meanwhile, Charlie needs to temporary storage the set of trapdoors for the verifying purpose. Upon receiving the search request, Bob divides each $T_{w'}$ into a sequence of symbols, performs search over the secure index I and returns a set of the document identifiers ID_{w_i}

and the value of r_1 of the node as *proof* as search result to Charlie. Note that the search will abort anytime in case the search is fail, in this case, only the *proof* of the current node will be return back. Charlie can retrieve the documents of his interest according to the document identifiers, and he can verify the correctness of search result by reconstructing the *proof* as described in Ref. [32].

Different from [32], in Ref. [38], each node is arranged a specific bloom filter as the *proof*, where the bloom filter of given node represents the current node and all its children. As a result, each internal node stores two attributes (r_0, r_1): r_0 stores the symbol value; r_1 stores a bloom filter and its signature, where the signature refers to the MAC of the bloom filter. At the leaf node, the *proof* is the symbol sequence of the corresponding keyword and its signature.

5.3 Verifiable Symmetric-Key PKS Using Twin Cloud

Recently, twin (hybrid) cloud architecture has attracted a lot of attentions. Bugiel *et al.* [40] provided architecture consists of twin cloud for secure outsourcing of data and arbitrary computations to an untrusted commodity cloud. Twin cloud architecture consists of a private cloud and a public cloud. The private cloud performs the security-critical operations, whereas the public cloud performs the performance-critical operations. For example, an enterprise might use a public cloud service, such as Amazon Simple Storage Service (Amazon S3) for archived data but continue to maintain in-house cloud for managing operational customer data.

Bugiel *et al.* [40] work inspired Wang *et al.* [32] to address the verifiable PKS in twin cloud architecture. As shown in Fig. 3.8, there are four entities defined in Ref. [32] system: the data owner, the user, the private cloud, and the public cloud. The key idea of this construction is to outsource the expensive operations (e.g., trapdoor generation and search result verification) to the private cloud and leave the lightweight computations to the user. Wang *et al.* [32] assume that the private cloud is "honest-but-curious" and the public cloud is "semi-honest-but-curious." Specifically, the private cloud will follow the proposed protocols honestly, but try to find out as much as secret information as possible based on their possessions, whereas the public cloud may not correctly follow the proposed protocol and forge part of the search result or execute only a fraction of searching operations honestly. In the proposed scheme, overhead operations such as index and trapdoor generations and search result verification are securely delegated

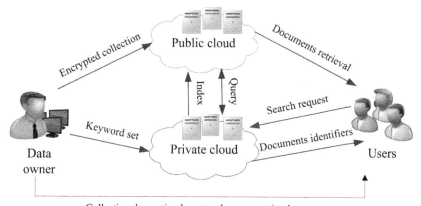

Figure 3.8 Architecture of verifiable PKS in twin cloud structure [32].

to the private cloud but leaves behind only the collection encryption and decryption at the data owner/user side.

More specifically, in Ref. [32], a data owner Alice outsources its encrypted collection to the public cloud and delegates the tasks of generating similarity keyword sets $\{S_{w_i,d}\}_{w_i \in W}$ and building the index to the private cloud. PKS requires a two-round interaction between an authorized user Charlie and the public cloud. In the first round, the private cloud works as a proxy between Charlie and the public cloud in order to allow Charlie to securely submit search queries that need to be evaluated. Specifically, upon receiving the search query from Charlie, the private cloud first translates it into a set of trapdoors and sends them to the public cloud. Upon receiving the set of trapdoors, the public cloud performs the search and returns the search result as set of encrypted document identifiers to the private cloud. Later, upon receiving the search outcomes from the public cloud, the private cloud performs decryption on them to obtain the documents identifiers as a plaintext form. Next, the private cloud performs verification on them to test whether the public cloud is honest, and then sends a set of document identifiers to Charlie. In the second round, Charlie can retrieve the documents of his interest according to the document identifiers from the public cloud.

5.4 LSH-Based PKS

Most PKS, such as [4,32,38], are specific to a particular distance measure (edit distance). Recently, Kuzu *et al.* [3] proposed a scheme provides more generic solution and it can be utilized for distinct similarity search contexts where LSH (formally defined in Section 2.3) is applicable.

Kuzu *et al.* [3] scheme offers efficient similarity tests and could easily be utilized for PKS. In this context, data items be the documents, features of the documents be the words in them, and query feature be a keyword. To enable efficient PKS, a data owner Alice builds a secure index I based on LSH for a document collection D with keys K_{id}, $K_{payload}$ (discussed in Section 4.3) and encrypts each document $d_i \in D$ with key K_{coll}, where $1 \le i \le n$, to form the encrypted collection C such that $C = (id_i, Enc_{K_{coll}}(d_i))_{1 \le i \le n}$, where id_i refers to the identifier of a document d_i. Next, she outsources the encrypted collection along with the secure index I to cloud owned by Bob. Alice shares the secret key used to encrypt the data collection K_{coll}, secret keys for index construction K_{id}, $K_{payload}$, metric space translation function ρ, and LSH function g of index construction with authorized users in order to allow them to selectively retrieve documents from cloud.

For a search keyword w, an authorized user Charlie first constructs a trapdoor for the keyword w. Specifically, he initially applies metric space translation on w ($\vec{w} = \rho(w)$). Then, he applies LSH to generate λ bucket labels as the plain query $(g_1(\vec{w}), \dots, g_\lambda(\vec{w}))$, where $g_i \in g$. Next, he encrypts the plain query to construct the trapdoor $T_w = \{\pi_{B_1}, \dots, \pi_{B_\lambda}\}$. Note that B_k refers to the kth bucket identifier. Finally, Charlie sends T_w to Bob.

Upon receiving the trapdoor, Bob performs search on the secure index I for each component of T_w and sends back to Charlie the corresponding encrypted λ buckets' bit vectors ($\{\sigma_{V_{B_i}} | (\pi_{B_i}, \sigma_{V_{B_i}}) \in I \land 1 \le i \le \lambda\}$). After that, Charlie scores the documents using the cumulative sum of all the retrieved bucket vectors. Based on these scores, Charlie sends the top t document identifiers to Bob to retrieve the relevant documents.

In order to hide the association between trapdoors and document identifiers, they used two servers (Bob and Tom) instead of single one under the assumption that both servers are "honest-but-curios" and do not collaborate with each other. Under this environment, Alice divides the outsourced information between two servers. Alice outsources the secure index I to Bob and encrypted collection C to Tom. The searching process will be a little different than a single server, Charlie sends its trapdoors T_w to Bob and received the corresponding encrypted bit vectors, ranks them locally, and sends the top t identifiers to Tom to receive the relevant documents.

Further, to minimize the computation overhead at Charlie, they utilize Paillier cryptosystem [41] to enable one-round search scheme for Charlie. We called this variation as "one-round multiservers." Under this setting,

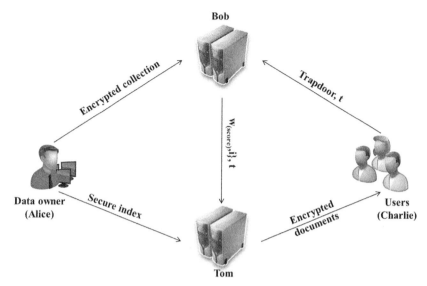

Figure 3.9 Architecture of PKS under one-round multiservers setting [3].

Alice first constructs a secure index I based on Paillier cryptosystem [3] and outsources the secure index I along with the Paillier public key K_{pub} to Bob, and the encrypted document collection C along with the Paillier private key K_{priv} to Tom. In Paillier-based secure index I, an encrypted form of each bit will be kept instead of a single encrypted bit vector in LSH-based secure index. To search, Charlie sends to Bob its trapdoor $T_w = \{\pi_1, \ldots, \pi_\lambda\}$ along with a parameter t (used for retrieval of documents with top t highest scores). Once Bob receives the trapdoor T_w, he extracts the payloads corresponding to all λ components of T_w and computes the scores $(w_{score}(i)_{1 \leq i \leq n})$ via homomorphic addition on encrypted bits. Next, Bob sends to Tom the $(w_{score}(i), i)$ pairs (encrypted scores with document identifiers i) along with the parameter t. Once Tom receives the information from Bob, he encrypts and ranks them, and then sends to Charlie the encrypted documents corresponding to the top t highest score. Figure 3.9 shows architecture of PKS under "one-round multiservers" setting.

5.5 B^{ed}-Tree Multi-PKS

So far, all discussed PKS schemes [3,4,13,30,32,38] support only a single PKS and do not support multi-PKS. That is, users may tend to provide a set of keywords instead of only one as the indicator of their search interest to retrieve the most relevant documents. For example, what if a user is interested in all documents that contain the keywords "private keyword search"? In this case, the user will need to conduct three searches with keywords "private," "keyword," and "search." Then, he/she will have to perform decryption of all the three returned results and do an intersection in order to extract the relevant documents that contain all three keywords "private keyword search." This process consumes communication bandwidth as well as additional decryption costs on the user side.

Chuah and Hu [27] propose PKS scheme based on B^{ed}-tree-based secure index (discussed in Section 4.4) that supports multi-keyword search. In Ref. [27], a data owner Alice first constructs a secure index I based on B^{ed}-tree and outsources the secure index I along with the encrypted collection to cloud owned by Bob. To search for a keyword $w =$ *"information retrieval,"* an authorized user Charlie submits a trapdoor consists of the following: $(v_w, h_w, d, H_{w,1}, \ldots, H_{w,k}, k)$ to Bob, where v_w is a data vector of the keyword w computed based on gram counting order, $h_w = h(w)$ refers to a hash value of the search keyword, where $h(.)$ denotes hash function, $H_{w,1}, \ldots, H_{w,k}$ denotes a set of hash values of the words included in the associated similarity keyword sets where $H_{w,j} = \bigcup_{w'_j \in S_{w,j}} h(w'_j)$ for $1 \leq j \leq k$, and k is desired edit distance that is tolerable to Charlie.

Upon receiving the search query, Bob will then search the secure index I to retrieve relevant keywords which are used to identify the documents containing these keywords. Specifically, Bob uses the data vector in the trapdoor v_w to search an entry in I. Bob iteratively searches the subtree from the corresponding pointers all the way to the leaf level of the tree. If v_w and the stored data vector at any leaf node has the edit distance that is within the edit distance bound, then the hash value in the trapdoor h_w is compared with the stored one in the leaf node to see if there is any match. In case there is a match, the set of stored encrypted document identifiers at this leaf node are sent back to Charlie. Otherwise, Bob determines if there is a match with any hash value in the trapdoor $\{H_{w,1}, \ldots, H_{w,k}\}$ can be found in the bloom filters stored at the leaf node, for example, $\{bf_{w_i,1}, \ldots, bf_{w_i,d}\}$. In case there is a match, the set of stored encrypted document identifiers at this leaf node are included in the response to be sent to Charlie. Finally, Charlie decrypts the search result and retrieves the relevant documents form Bob.

5.6 Public-Key PKS

In the literature, many schemes have been designed for PKS in symmetric-key cryptosystem; however, there exist only a few schemes in public-key cryptosystem. Dong *et al.* [36] propose a public-key PKS based on homomorphic encryption scheme [42] and Hamming distance as the distance measurement. In Ref. [36], the cloud server is able to build a bilinear-based inverted index over encrypted collection without knowing the encrypted keywords.

In Ref. [36], a sender wishes to send a document d_i to a client. He/she first extracts the set of keywords $W_i = \{w_{i_1}, \ldots, w_{i_z}\}$ and sends a request contains the following tuples $\{s_{a_j}, s_{b_j}, IPEFKS(\text{pk}, w_{i_j})\}_{1 \leq j \leq z}$ along with the document identifier id_i and the encrypted document d_i to a cloud owned by Bob, where s_{a_j}, s_{b_j} is the corresponding term for the jth keyword in ciphertext which used by the cloud to build an secure index without disclosing the keywords privacy, *IPEFKS* is the keyword encryption algorithm which formally defined in Ref. [36], and pk is the client's public key.

Upon receiving the request from the sender, Bob builds a bilinear-based secure index I (described in Section 4.5). Next, consider a client, who wished to retrieve documents containing keywords with a certain Hamming distance threshold th compared with his interested keyword w, he/she computes first a trapdoor and sends it to Bob. Upon receiving the search request, Bob computes the encrypted result ER_w using homomorphic encryption scheme [42]. Next, Bob sends the encrypted result back to client, who then performs retrieve operation with Bob. Specifically, given a private key sk, the encrypted result ER_w of the keyword w, and the Hamming distance threshold th, the retrieve process outputs *YES* if $hd(w, w_{i_j}) <$ th, where $w_{i_j} \in W_i$ and hd(.) denotes a Hamming distance, otherwise, outputs *NO*.

5.7 Classification

As shown in Tables 3.1 and 3.2, we classify PKS over encrypted document collection based on the cryptosystem structure of the encryption algorithms (symmetric key and public key) and which technique used to construct the similarity keyword set (enumerating, wildcard) and the secure index (inverted index based, symbol-trie based, LSH based, B^{ed}-tree based, bilinear based). Here, we only consider a set of representative or well-known PKS schemes that are discussed in this chapter, and it is not intended to be a full list of all the existing PKS over encrypted document collection schemes.

6. CONCLUSION

Due to cost-efficiency and less hands-on management, data owners are outsourcing their data to the cloud which can provide access to the

Table 3.1 Classification Based on Encryption Algorithms

| | Cryptosystem | |
Scheme	Symmetric Key	Public Key
Li *et al.* [4]	✓	✗
Li *et al.* [13]	✓	✗
Wang *et al.* [30]	✓	✗
Wang *et al.* [32]	✓	✗
Kuzu *et al.* [3]	✓	✗
Chuah and Hu [27]	✓	✗
Dong *et al.* [36]	✗	✓

Table 3.2 Classification Based on Similarity Keyword Sets and Indexing Construction Techniques

Scheme	Similarity Keyword Set Techniques	Indexing Techniques
Li *et al.* [4]	Enumerating and wildcard	Inverted index based
Li *et al.* [13]	Enumerating and Wildcard	Symbol-trie based
Wang *et al.* [30]	Wildcard	Symbol-trie based
Wang *et al.* [32]	Wildcard	Symbol-trie based
Kuzu *et al.* [3]	N/A	LSH based and Paillier based
Chuah and Hu [27]	Wildcard	B^{ed}-tree based
Dong *et al.* [36]	N/A	Bilinear based

data as a service. However, by outsourcing their data to the cloud, the data owners lose control over their data as the cloud provider becomes a third-party service provider. At first, data encryption protects the confidentiality of the outsourced data from third-party providers such as cloud as well as from the intruders in the case of a successful attack on the cloud. However, encryption adds another complexity layer and makes the utilization/management of encrypted data challenging. Especially, the problem of query processing over encrypted data without ever decrypting it is not trivial. PKS is a problem of fundamental importance for a wide array of fields, including databases and data mining. It allows a user to search for the most similar objects to his/her request over encrypted data without nothing be leaked beyond the search and access patterns. In this work, we focused on PKS over encrypted document collection. Consider a data owner outsources a document collection $D = \{d_1, \ldots, d_n\}$ to cloud in encrypted form $C = \{c_1, \ldots, c_n\}$ such that any authorized user, including data owner, can search the collection C at cloud while hiding information about the collection and queries from cloud. Given a keyword

w with a similarity metric d, PKS intends to find the encrypted documents containing keywords that are within a certain similarity metric d from w in privacy preserving manner. We provided a comprehensive literature survey on the existing schemes that can be used to conduct PKS over encrypted outsourced document collection to cloud. Also, we classified the existing schemes based on various important parameters in order to make it easier for users to select the best scheme depending on his/her application requirements.

It's worth pointing out that the main contribution of the discussed schemes in this chapter was to come up with practical and effective PKS schemes with regard to both storage and search efficiency by proposing different techniques such as enumeration and wildcard approaches to construct storage-efficient similarity keyword sets and exploring different data structures such as variety of indexing algorithms to enhance the search time.

REFERENCES

[1] H. Hu, J. Xu, C. Ren, B. Choi, Processing private queries over untrusted data cloud through privacy homomorphism, in: IEEE 27th International Conference on Data Engineering, IEEE, 2011, pp. 601–612.
[2] P. Mell, T. Grance, The nist definition of cloud computing (draft), NIST special publication 800 (145) (2011) 7.
[3] M. Kuzu, M. S. Islam, M. Kantarcioglu, Efficient similarity search over encrypted data, in: Data Engineering (ICDE), 2012 IEEE 28th International Conference on, IEEE, 2012, pp. 1156–1167.
[4] J. Li, Q. Wang, C. Wang, N. Cao, K. Ren, W. Lou, Fuzzy keyword search over encrypted data in cloud computing, in: INFOCOM, 2010 Proceedings IEEE, IEEE, 2010, pp. 1–5.
[5] H. Hacıgümüş, B. Hore, B. Iyer, S. Mehrotra, Search on encrypted data, in: T. Yu, S. Jajodia (Eds.), Secure Data Management in Decentralized Systems, ser. Advances in Information Security, vol. 33, Springer, US, 2007, pp. 383–425.
[6] C. Wang, N. Cao, J. Li, K. Ren, W. Lou, Secure ranked keyword search over encrypted cloud data, in: Distributed Computing Systems (ICDCS), 2010 IEEE 30th International Conference on, IEEE, 2010, pp. 253–262.
[7] K. Ren, C. Wang, Q. Wang, Toward secure and effective data utilization in public cloud, Network, IEEE 26 (6) (2012) 69–74.
[8] E.-J. Goh, Secure indexes, Tech. rep., Cryptology ePrint Archive, Report 2003/216 (2003).
[9] Y.-C. Chang, M. Mitzenmacher, Privacy preserving keyword searches on remote encrypted data, in: J. Ioannidis, A. Keromytis, M. Yung (Eds.), Applied Cryptography and Network Security, ser. Lecture Notes in Computer Science, vol. 3531, Springer, Berlin Heidelberg, 2005, pp. 442–455.
[10] R. Curtmola, J. Garay, S. Kamara, R. Ostrovsky, Searchable symmetric encryption: improved definitions and efficient constructions, in: Proceedings of the 13th ACM conference on Computer and communications security, ACM, 2006, pp. 79–88.

[11] D. Boneh, G. Di Crescenzo, R. Ostrovsky, G. Persiano, Public key encryption with keyword search, in: C. Cachin, J. Camenisch (Eds.), Advances in Cryptology-Eurocrypt 2004, ser. Lecture Notes in Computer Science, vol. 3027, Springer, Berlin Heidelberg, 2004, pp. 506–522.

[12] D. Boneh, B. Waters, Conjunctive, subset, and range queries on encrypted data, in: Theory of cryptography, Springer, 2007, pp. 535–554.

[13] J. Li, Q. Wang, C. Wang, N. Cao, K. Ren, W. Lou, Enabling efficient fuzzy keyword search over encrypted data in cloud computing.

[14] C. D. Manning, P. Raghavan, H. Schütze, Introduction to information retrieval, Vol. 1, Cambridge: University Press Cambridge, 2008.

[15] D. X. Song, D. Wagner, A. Perrig, Practical techniques for searches on encrypted data, in: Security and Privacy, 2000. S&P 2000. Proceedings. 2000 IEEE Symposium on, IEEE, 2000, pp. 44–55.

[16] Q. Tang, Search in encrypted data: Theoretical models and practical applications, IACR Cryptology ePrint Archive 2012 (2012) 648.

[17] X. Pang, B. Yang, Q. Huang, Privacy-preserving noisy keyword search in cloud computing, in: T. Chim, T. Yuen (Eds.), Information and Communications Security, ser. Lecture Notes in Computer Science, vol. 7618, Springer, Berlin Heidelberg, 2012, pp. 154–166.

[18] C. Wang, Q. Wang, K. Ren, Towards secure and effective utilization over encrypted cloud data, in: Proceedings of the 31st International Conference on Distributed Computing Systems Workshops, ser. ICDCSW '11, IEEE Computer Society, Washington, DC, USA, 2011, pp. 282–286.

[19] A. Arriaga, Q. Tang, P. Ryan, Trapdoor privacy in asymmetric searchable encryption schemes, in: D. Pointcheval, D. Vergnaud (Eds.), Progress in Cryptology-AFRICACRYPT 2014, ser. Lecture Notes in Computer Science, vol. 8469, Springer, Berlin Heidelberg, 2014, pp. 31–50.

[20] J. Baek, R. Safavi-Naini, W. Susilo, Public key encryption with keyword search revisited, in: Computational Science and Its Applications–ICCSA 2008, Springer, 2008, pp. 1249–1259.

[21] Q. Tang, L. Chen, Public-key encryption with registered keyword search, in: F. Martinelli, B. Preneel (Eds.), Public Key Infrastructures, Services and Applications, ser. Lecture Notes in Computer Science, vol. 6391, Springer, Berlin Heidelberg, 2010, pp. 163–178.

[22] A. J. Menezes, P. C. Van Oorschot, S. A. Vanstone, Handbook of applied cryptography, CRC press, 2010.

[23] R. Sakai, S. Mitsunari, M. Kasahara, Cryptographic schemes based on pairing over elliptic curve., IEIC Technical Report (Institute of Electronics, Information and Communication Engineers) 101 (214) (2001) 75–80.

[24] O. Goldreich, The foundations of cryptography, volume 2, chapter 7 (2004).

[25] Y. Huang, J. Katz, D. Evans, Quid-pro-quo-tocols: strengthening semi-honest protocols with dual execution, in: Proceedings of the 2012 IEEE Symposium on Security and Privacy, ser. SP '12, IEEE Computer Society, Washington, DC, USA, 2012, pp. 272–284.

[26] Z. Zhang, M. Hadjieleftheriou, B. C. Ooi, D. Srivastava, Bed-tree: an all-purpose index structure for string similarity search based on edit distance, in: Proceedings of the 2010 ACM SIGMOD International Conference on Management of data, ser. SIGMOD '10, ACM, New York, NY, USA, 2010, pp. 915–926.

[27] M. Chuah, W. Hu, Privacy-aware bedtree based solution for fuzzy multi-keyword search over encrypted data, in: Distributed Computing Systems Workshops (ICDCSW), 2011 31st International Conference on, IEEE, 2011, pp. 273–281.

[28] P. Indyk, R. Motwani, Approximate nearest neighbors: towards removing the curse of dimensionality, in: Proceedings of the thirtieth annual ACM symposium on Theory of computing, ser. STOC '98, ACM, New York, NY, USA, 1998, pp. 604–613.

[29] A. Gionis, P. Indyk, R. Motwani, et al., Similarity search in high dimensions via hashing, in: VLDB, Vol. 99, 1999, pp. 518–529.

[30] C. Wang, K. Ren, S. Yu, K. M. R. Urs, Achieving usable and privacy-assured similarity search over outsourced cloud data, in: INFOCOM, 2012 Proceedings IEEE, IEEE, 2012, pp. 451–459.

[31] S. Heinz, J. Zobel, H. E. Williams, Burst tries: a fast, efficient data structure for string keys, ACM Transactions on Information Systems (TOIS) 20 (2) (2002) 192–223.

[32] J. Wang, H. Ma, Q. Tang, J. Li, H. Zhu, S. Ma, X. Chen, Efficient verifiable fuzzy keyword search over encrypted data in cloud computing, Computer Science and Information Systems 10 (2) (2013) 667–684.

[33] C. Faloutsos, K. Lin, FastMap: A fast algorithm for indexing, data-mining and visualization of traditional and multimedia datasets, in: Proceedings of the 1995 ACM SIGMOD International Conference on Management of Data, vol. 24, New York, NY, USA: ACM, 1995.

[34] J. Qin, W. Wang, C. Xiao, Y. Lu, X. Lin, H. Wang, Asymmetric signature schemes for efficient exact edit similarity query processing.

[35] F. Zhang, R. Safavi-Naini, W. Susilo, An efficient signature scheme from bilinear pairings and its applications, Public Key Cryptography–PKC 2004, Springer, 2004, pp. 277–290.

[36] Q. Dong, Z. Guan, L. Wu, Z. Chen, Fuzzy keyword search over encrypted data in the public key setting, in: J. Wang, H. Xiong, Y. Ishikawa, J. Xu, J. Zhou (Eds.), Web-Age Information Management, ser. Lecture Notes in Computer Science, vol. 7923, Springer, Berlin Heidelberg, 2013, pp. 729–740.

[37] J. Bringer, H. Chabanne, Embedding edit distance to enable private keyword search, Human-centric Computing and Information Sciences 2 (1) (2012) 1–12.

[38] J. Wang, H. Ma, Q. Tang, J. Li, H. Zhu, S. Ma, X. Chen, A new efficient verifiable fuzzy keyword search scheme, Journal of Wireless Mobile Networks, Ubiquitous Computing and Dependable Applications 3 (4) (2012) 61–71.

[39] Q. Chai, G. Gong, Verifiable symmetric searchable encryption for semi-honest-but-curious cloud servers, in: Proceedings of IEEE International Conference on Communications (ICC 2012), IEEE, Ottawa, ON, Canada, 2012, pp. 917–922.

[40] S. Bugiel, S. Nürnberger, A.-R. Sadeghi, T. Schneider, Twin clouds: An architecture for secure cloud computing, in: Workshop on Cryptography and Security in Clouds (WCSC 2011), Zürich, Switzerland 2011.

[41] P. Paillier, Public-key cryptosystems based on composite degree residuosity classes, in: J. Stern (Ed.), Advances in cryptology EUROCRYPT 99, ser. Lecture Notes in Computer Science, vol. 1592, Springer, Berlin Heidelberg, 1999, pp. 223–238.

[42] J. Fan, F. Vercauteren, Somewhat practical fully homomorphic encryption., IACR Cryptology ePrint Archive 2012 (2012) 144.

ABOUT THE AUTHORS

Yousef Elmehdwi received his bachelor's degree in Computer Science from Benghazi University, Libya in 1993 and MSc degree in Information Technology from the Mannheim University of Applied Science, Germany in 2005. Elmehdwi has joined the Computer Science Department at the Missouri University of Science and Technology, Rolla, Missouri, as a graduate student in January 2010. He is currently working toward his PhD degree under the supervision of Dr. Wei Jiang. His research interests lie at the crossroads of privacy, security, and data mining with current focus on privacy-preserving query processing over encrypted data outsourced to cloud.

Dr. Wei Jiang is an assistant professor at the Department of Computer Science of Missouri University of Science and Technology. He received the bachelor's degrees in both Computer Science and Mathematics from the University of Iowa, Iowa City, Iowa, in 2002. He received the master's degree in Computer Science and the Ph.D. degree from Purdue University, West Lafayette, IN, in 2004 and 2008, respectively. His research interests include privacy-preserving data mining, data integration, privacy issues in federated search environments, and text sanitization. His research has been funded by the National Science Foundation, the Office of Naval Research, and University of the Missouri Research Board.

Alireza Hurson is currently a professor of Computer Science Department at Missouri S&T. For the period of 2008–2012, he chaired Computer Science Department. Before joining Missouri S&T, he was a professor of Computer Science and Engineering Department at The Pennsylvania State University. His research for the past three decades has been directed toward the design and analysis of general as well as special purpose computer architectures. His research has been supported by NSF, DARPA, Department of Education, Air Force, Office of Naval Research, Oak Ridge National Laboratory, NCR Corp., General Electric, IBM, Lockheed Martin, Penn State University, and Missouri S&T. He has published over 300 technical papers in areas including database systems, multidatabases, global information sharing, application of mobile agent technology, object-oriented databases, mobile computing environment, sensor and ad hoc networks, computer architecture and cache memory, parallel and distributed processing, dataflow architectures, and VLSI algorithms. Dr. Hurson has been the coauthor of five IEEE tutorial books and editor of 10 volumes of *Advances in Computers*. Hurson is the cofounder of the *IEEE Symposium on Parallel and Distributed Processing (currently IPDPS)*, *IEEE Conference on Pervasive Computing and Communications (PerCom)*, and *IEEE International Green Computing Conference (IGCC)*.

CHAPTER FOUR

Multiobjective Optimization for Software Refactoring and Evolution

Ali Ouni[*,†], Marouane Kessentini[†], Houari Sahraoui[*]
[*]DIRO, University of Montreal, Montreal, Quebec, Canada
[†]CIS, SBSE Research Laboratory, University of Michigan, Michigan, USA

Contents

Advances in Computers, Volume 94
ISSN 0065-2458
http://dx.doi.org/10.1016/B978-0-12-800161-5.00004-9
103

Abstract

Many studies reported that software maintenance, traditionally defined as any modification made on a software system after its delivery, consumes up to 90% of the total cost of a typical software project. Adding new functionalities, correcting bugs, and modifying the code to improve its quality are major parts of those costs. To ease these maintenance activities, one of the most used techniques is the *refactoring* which improves design structure while preserving the external behavior.

In general, refactoring is performed through two main steps: (1) detection of code fragments corresponding to design defects that need to be improved/fixed and (2) identification of refactoring solutions to achieve this goal. Our research project targets the automation of these two refactoring steps. Concretely, we consider the detection step as a search-based process to find the suitable detection rules for each type of design defect, by means of a genetic algorithm. To guide the rule-derivation process, real examples of design defects are used. For the refactoring identification step, a multiobjective search-based approach is also used. The process aims at finding the optimal sequence of refactoring operations that improve the software quality by minimizing the number of detected defects. In addition, we explore other objectives to optimize: the effort needed to apply refactorings, semantic preservation, and the similarity with good refactorings applied in the past to similar contexts. Hence, the effort corresponds to the code modification/adaptation score needed to apply the suggested refactoring solutions. On the other hand, the semantic preservation insures that the refactored program is semantically equivalent to the original one, and that it models correctly the domain semantics. Indeed, we use knowledge from historical code changes to propose new refactoring solutions in similar contexts to improve the automation of refactoring.

LIST OF ABBREVIATIONS

CC Code change score
CD Cohesion-based dependency
DCR Defect correction ratio
DS Dependency-based similarity
EC Extract class
EI Extract interface
EM Extract method
FIU Feature inheritance usefulness
GA Genetic algorithm
GP Genetic programming
IC Inline class
IS Implementation-based similarity
MC Move class
MF Move field
MM Move method
MOGA Multiobjective genetic algorithm
NSGA-II Nondominated sorting genetic algorithm
PDF Push-down field
PDM Push-down method
PUF Pull-up field
PUM Pull-up method
Q Quality
RC Recorded refactorings
RP Refactoring precision
RR Refactoring reuse
RS Random search
S Semantics
VS Vocabulary-based similarity

1. INTRODUCTION

1.1 Research Context

Software maintenance is defined in IEEE Standard 1219 [1] as: The modification of a software product after delivery to correct faults, to improve performance or other attributes, or to adapt the product to a modified environment. A startling 90% of the cost of a typical software system is incurred during the maintenance phase [2]. Improving the quality of existing software will drastically improve productivity and competitiveness of our software industry.

Improving the quality of software induces the detection and correction of design defects. Typically, design defects refer to design situations that adversely affect the development of software. As stated by Fenton and Pfleeger [3], design defects are unlikely to cause failures directly, but may do it indirectly. In general, they make a system difficult to change, which may often introduce bugs. The most well-known example of defects is the *blob* (found in designs where one large class monopolizes the behavior of a system and other classes primarily encapsulate data). Thus, design defects should be identified and corrected by the development team as early as possible for maintainability and evolution considerations.

1.2 Problem Statement

Detecting and fixing design defects are still, to some extent, a difficult, time-consuming, error-prone, and manual process. As a consequence, automating design defects detection and correction is considered as a very challenging software engineering task.

The defect detection process consists of finding code fragments that violate common object-oriented principles (structure or semantic properties) on code elements such as the ones involving coupling and complexity. In fact, the common idea in existing contributions [4–6] consists of defining rules manually to identify key symptoms that characterize a defect using combinations of mainly quantitative, structural, and/or lexical information. However, in an exhaustive scenario, the number of possible defects to manually characterize with rules can be very large. On the other hand, other work [7] proposes to generate detection rules using formal definitions of defects. Although this partial automation of rule writing helps developers basing on symptom description, still, translating symptoms into rules is not obvious because there is no consensus of defining design defects based on their symptoms [8]. In the next section, we highlight the different design defects detection and correction challenges.

Once design defects are detected, they need to be fixed. To correct detected defects, one of the most used techniques is the refactoring which improves design structure while preserving the external behavior [8]. Opdyke [9] defines refactoring as the process of improving a code after it has been written by changing its internal structure without changing the external behavior. The idea is to reorganize variables, classes, and methods in order to facilitate future extensions. This reorganization is used to improve different aspects of software quality: reusability, maintainability, and complexity [9]. Roughly speaking, we can identify two distinct steps in the refactoring process: (1) detect when a program should be refactored and (2) identify which refactorings should be applied and where [10]. For example, after detecting a blob defect, many refactoring operations can be used to reduce the number of functionalities in a specific class, such as move methods and extract class. In the best of our knowledge, most of the existing contributions suggest refactorings with the perspective of improving only some design/quality metrics. However, this could not be enough to obtain good refactoring solutions. Hence, to obtain good refactoring strategies, other considerations have to be targeted such as the correction effort minimization, semantic preservation, and the similarity with good refactorings applied/recorded in the past in similar contexts.

In the next subsections, we highlight the different problems addressed in this research work that are mainly related to the design defects detection and correction.

1.2.1 Automating Defects Detection

Although there is a substantial amount of research work focusing on the detection of design defects [3–5,7–9,11], there are many open issues that need to be addressed when defining a detection strategy. In the following, we highlight these open issues.

Problem 1.1. Most of the existing approaches are based on translating symptoms into rules. However, there is a difference between detecting symptoms and asserting that the detected situation is an actual defect.

Problem 1.2. There is no consensus on the definition of design defects based on their symptoms. Although when consensus exists, the same symptom could be associated to many defect types, which may compromise the precise identification of defect types.

Problem 1.3. The majority of existing detection methods do not provide an efficient manner to guide a manual inspection of candidate defects. Indeed, the process of manually defining detection rules, understanding the defect candidates, selecting the true positives, and correcting them is very long, fastidious, and not always profitable.

Problem 1.4. Existing approaches require an expert to manually write and validate detection rules.

1.2.2 Automating Defects Correction

Detected defects can be fixed by applying the suitable refactoring operations [12]. Although there exist several works on software refactoring [13–17], until now, they do not provide an efficient and fully automated approach. Therefore, several open issues should be addressed when searching for refactoring solutions to improve the software quality (i.e., defects correction). Hence, several problems need to be addressed.

Problem 2.1. The majority of existing approaches [9,18,19] have manually defined "standard" refactorings for each defect type to remove its symptoms. However, it is difficult to define "standard" refactorings for each defect type and to generalize it because generally it depends on the programs in their context.

Problem 2.2. Removing defect symptoms does not mean that the defect is corrected, and in the majority of cases, these "standard" solutions are enable to remove all symptoms for each defect.

Problem 2.3. Different correction strategies should be defined for the same type of defect. The problem is how to find the "best" refactoring solutions from a large list of candidate refactoring operations and how to combine them in a suitable order? The list of all possible correction strategies, for each defect type, can be very large [12]. Thus, the process of defining correction strategies manually, from an exhaustive list of refactorings, is time-consuming and error-prone.

Problem 2.4. In the majority of existing approaches [13,14,16,20], the code quality can be improved without fixing design defects (i.e., improving some quality metrics does not guarantee that detected defects are fixed). Therefore, the link between defect detection (refactoring opportunities) and correction is not obvious. In other terms, we need to ensure whether the refactoring concretely corrects detected defects.

Problem 2.5. Existing approaches consider the refactoring (i.e., the correction process) as local process by correcting defects (or improving quality) separately. In fact, a refactoring solution should not be specific to only one defect type and the correction process should consider the impact of refactoring. For example, moving methods to reduce the size/complexity of a class may increase the global coupling.

Problem 2.6. Reduce the refactoring effort (code adaptation/ modification effort). Hence, improving software quality and reducing the effort are complementary and sometimes conflicting considerations. In some cases, correcting some defects corresponds to reimplementing a large portion of the system. In fact, a refactoring solution that fixes all defects is not necessarily the optimal one due to the high adaptation/modification effort needed.

Problem 2.7. In general, refactoring restructures a program to improve its structure without altering its behavior. However, it is challenging to preserve the domain semantics of a program when refactoring is decided/implemented automatically. Indeed, a program could be syntactically correct, and have the right behavior, but still model incorrectly the domain semantics. We need to preserve the rationale behind why and how code elements are grouped and connected when applying refactoring operations to improve code quality.

All of these observations are at the origin of the work conducted in the scope of this research work. In the next section, we give an overview and our research direction to solve the above-mentioned problems.

1.3 Proposed Solutions

To address the above-mentioned problems, we propose the following solutions which are organized into three principal contributions.

Contribution 1: Design defects detection To automate the detection of design defects, we propose a search-based approach [21] using genetic algorithm (GA) to automatically generate detection rules. To this end, knowledge from defect examples is used to generate detection rules. The detection process takes as inputs a base (i.e., a set) of defect examples and takes as controlling parameters a set of quality metrics (the usefulness of these metrics was defined and discussed in the literature [22]). This step generates a set of design defects detection rules. Consequently, a solution to the defect detection problem is represented as a set of rules that best detect the defects presented on the base of examples with high score of precision and recall.

Contribution 2: Design defects correction To correct the detected defects, we need to find the suitable refactoring solution. A refactoring solution is a combination of refactoring operations. To overcome the list of problems stated previously, we divide our contribution into four substeps.

Contribution 2.1. As a first step, we consider the process of generating correction solutions as a single-objective optimization problem. A correction solution is defined as a combination of refactoring operations that should minimize, as much as possible, the number of detected defects using the detection rules. To this end, we use GA [23] to find and suggest the best combination of refactoring operations from a large list of available refactorings [24].

Contribution 2.2. Then, we extend this contribution, to see the refactoring process as a multiobjective optimization problem. We define a "good" refactoring solution as the combination of refactoring operations that should maximize as much as possible the number of corrected defects with minimal code modification/adaptation effort (i.e., the cost of applying the refactoring sequence) [21]. The idea is to find the best compromise between maximizing quality and minimizing code adaptability effort. Thus, the aim is to reduce the complexity of the suggested refactorings by achieving meaningful reductions in terms of code modifications score. Indeed, this contribution does not correct defects separately since we consider the correction as a global process instead of local one. In addition, we do not need to define an exhaustive list of defects and to specify standard refactoring for each defect type.

Contribution 2.3. As a third step, it is challenging to integrate the semantic preservation especially that refactoring solutions are decided automatically using our search-based approach. In fact, a program could be syntactically correct, have the right behavior, but model incorrectly the domain semantics. One of the key issues we need to solve is to approximate the semantic similarity between code fragments because the semantics is not clearly defined in the code. In this contribution, we propose a multiobjective optimization approach to find the best sequence of refactorings that maximizes quality improvements (i.e., minimize the number of defects) and at the same time minimizes potential semantic errors. To this end, we use the nondominated sorting genetic algorithm (NSGA-II) to find the best compromise between these two conflicting objectives [25]. In nutshell, this contribution shows how to automatically suggest refactoring solution in a way that preserves as much as possible the semantics of the original software system.

Contribution 2.4. To improve the automaton of refactoring, we start from the observation that recorded/historical code changes could be used to propose new refactoring solutions in similar contexts. In addition, this knowledge can be combined with structural and semantic information to improve the automation of refactoring. In this contribution, we propose a multiobjective optimization to find the compromise between all of the mentioned objectives. We define "optimal" refactoring solutions as the sequence of refactorings that provide the right balance between minimizing the number of defects, minimizing the number of code changes needed to apply the refactorings, minimizing semantic errors, and maximizing the use of refactorings applied in the past to similar contexts [26].

To conclude, our contribution is built on the idea that a "good" refactoring solution should minimize, as much as possible, the number of detected defects, with minimal code changes, while preserving the domain semantics of the original program and maintaining the consistency with the development/maintenance history.

2. RELATED WORK

In this section, we bring the state of the art of existing work related to our research area, and we highlight the open research problems for the research community. Hence, the related work can be divided broadly into two research areas: (1) detection of design defects and (2) correction of design defects. These topics are discussed below.

2.1 Detection of Design Defects

There has been much research effort focusing on the study of maintainability defects, also called anomalies [8], antipatterns [9], or smells [3] in the literature. Such defects include, for example, the blob (very large class), spaghetti code (SC) (tangled control structure), and functional decomposition (FD) (a class representing only a single function).

Existing approaches for design defects detection can be classified into six broad categories: manual approaches, symptom-based approaches, rule-based approaches, probabilistic approaches, machine learning-based approaches, and visualization-based approaches.

2.1.1 Manual Approaches

In the literature, the first book that has been specially written for design smells was by Brown *et al.* [8] which provide broad spectrum and large views on design smells, and antipatterns that aimed at a wide audience for academic community as well as in industry. Indeed, in Ref. [9], Fowler *et al.* have described a list of design smells which may possibly exist on a program. They suggested that software maintainers should manually inspect the program to detect existing design smells. In addition, they specify particular refactorings for each defect type. Travassos *et al.* [27] have also proposed a manual approach for detecting defects in object-oriented designs. The idea is to create a set of "reading techniques" which help a reviewer to "read" a design artifact for the purpose of finding relevant information. These reading techniques give specific and practical guidance for identifying defects in object-oriented designs. So that each reading technique helps the maintainer focusing on some aspects of the design, in such way that an inspection team applying the entire family should achieve a high degree of coverage of the design defects. In addition, in Ref. [28], another proposed approach is based on violations of design rules and guidelines. This approach consists of analyzing legacy code, specifying frequent design problems as queries, and locating the occurrences of these problems in a model derived from the source code. However, the majority of the detected problems were simple ones, since it is based on simple conditions with particular threshold values. As a consequence, this approach did not address complex design defects.

The main disadvantage of exiting manual approaches is that they are ultimately a human-centric process that requires a great human effort and strong analysis and interpretation effort from software maintainers to find design fragments that correspond to defects. In addition, these techniques are time-consuming, error-prone and depend on programs in their contexts. Another important issue is that locating defects manually has been described as more a human intuition than an exact science. To circumvent the above-mentioned problems, some semiautomated approaches have emerged.

2.1.2 Symptom-Based Detection

Moha *et al.* [7] started by describing defect symptoms using a domain-specific language (DSL) for their approach called DECOR. They proposed a consistent vocabulary and DSL to specify antipatterns based on the review of existing work on design defects found in the literature. To describe defect symptoms, different notions are involved, such as class roles and structures. Symptoms descriptions are later mapped to detection algorithms. However, converting symptoms into rules needs a significant analysis and interpretation effort to find the suitable threshold values. In addition, this approach uses heuristics to approximate some notions which result in an important rate of false positives. Indeed, this approach has been evaluated on only four well-known design defects: the Blob, FD, SC, and Swiss-army knife because the literature provides obvious symptom descriptions on these defects. Similarly, Munro [4] have proposed description and symptoms-based approach using a precise definition of bad smells from the informal descriptions given by the originators Fowler and Beck [9]. The characteristics of design defects have been used to systematically define a set of measurements and interpretation rules for a subset of design defects as a template form. This template consists of three main parts: a code smell name, a text-based description of its characteristics, and heuristics for its detection.

The major limitation of symptoms-based approaches is that there exists no consensus in defining symptoms. A defect may have several and different interpretations by a maintainer. Another limitation is that for an exhaustive list of defects, the number of possible defects to be manually described, characterized with rules and mapped to detection algorithms can be very large. Indeed, the background and knowledge of maintainers affect their understanding of defects, given a set of symptoms. As a consequence, symptoms-based approaches are also considered as time-consuming and error-prone. Thus, automating the detection of design defects is still a real challenge.

2.1.3 Metric-Based Approaches

The idea to automate the problem of design defects detection is not new, neither is the idea to use quality metrics to improve the quality of software systems.

Marinescu [29] have proposed a mechanism called "detection strategy" for formulating metrics-based rules that capture deviations from good design principles and heuristics. Detection strategies allow to a maintainer to directly locate classes or methods affected by a particular design defect. As such, Marinescu has defined detection strategies for capturing around 10 important flaws of object-oriented design found in the literature. After his suitable symptom-based characterization of design defects, Munro [4] proposed metric-based heuristics for detecting defects, which are similar to Marinescu's detection strategies. Munro has also performed an empirical study to justify his choice of metrics and thresholds for detecting smells. Salehie et al. [30] proposed a metric-based heuristic framework to detect and locate object-oriented design flaws similar to those illustrated by Marinescu [29]. It is accomplished by evaluating design quality of an object-oriented system through quantifying deviations from good design heuristics and principles by mapping these design flaws to class-level metrics such as complexity, coupling, and cohesion by defining rules. Erni et al. [31] introduce the concept of multimetrics, as an n-tuple of metrics expressing a quality criterion (e.g., modularity). Unfortunately, multimetrics neither encapsulate metrics in a more abstract construct, nor do they allow a flexible combination of metrics.

In general, the effectiveness of combining metric/threshold is not obvious. That is, for each defect, rules that are expressed in terms of metric combinations need a significant calibration effort to find the fitting threshold values for each metric. Since there exists no consensus in defining design smells, different threshold values should be tested to find the best ones.

2.1.4 Probabilistic Approaches

Probabilistic approaches represent another way for detecting defects. Alikacem *et al.* [11] have considered the defects detection process as fuzzy-logic problem, using rules with fuzzy labels for metrics, e.g., small, medium, and large. To this end, they proposed a DSL that allows the specification of fuzzy-logic rules that include quantitative properties and relationships among classes. The thresholds for quantitative properties are replaced by fuzzy labels. Hence, when evaluating the rules, actual metric values are mapped to truth values for the labels by means of membership functions that are obtained by fuzzy clustering. Although fuzzy inference allows to explicitly handle the uncertainty of the detection process and ranks the candidates, authors did not validate their approach on real programs. Recently, another probabilistic approach has been proposed by Khomh *et al.* [32] extending the DECOR approach [7], a symptom-based approach, to support uncertainty and to sort the defect candidates accordingly. This approach is managed by Bayesian belief network (BBN) that implements the detection rules of DECOR. The detection outputs are probabilities that a class is an occurrence of a defect type, i.e., the degree of uncertainty for a class to be a defect. They also showed that BBNs can be calibrated using historical data from both similar and different context.

Although, in probabilistic approaches, the above-mentioned problems in Chapter 1 related to the use of rules and metrics/thresholds do not arise, it still suffers from the problem of selecting the suitable metrics to conduct a detection process.

2.1.5 Machine Learning-Based Approaches

Machine learning represents another alternative for detecting design defects. Catal *et al.* [33] used different machine learning algorithms to predict defective modules. They investigated the effect of dataset size, metrics set, and feature selection techniques for software fault prediction problem. They employed several algorithms based on artificial immune systems (AISs). Kessentini *et al.* [34] have proposed an automated approach for discovering design defects. The detection is based on the idea that the more code deviates from good practices, the more likely it is bad. Taking inspiration from AIS, this approach learns from examples of well-designed and implemented software elements, to estimate the risks of classes to deviate from "normality," i.e., a set of classes representing "good" design that conforms to object-oriented principles. Elements of assessed systems that diverge from normality to detectors are considered as risky. Although this approach succeeded in discovering risky code, it does not provide a mechanism to identify the type of the detected defect. Similarly, Hassaine *et al.* [5] have proposed an approach for detecting design smells using machine learning technique inspired from the AIS. Their approach is designed to systematically detect classes whose characteristics violate some established design rules. Rules are inferred from sets of manually validated examples of defects reported in the literature and freely available.

The major benefit of machine learning-based approaches is that it does not require great experts' knowledge and interpretation. In addition, they succeeded to some extent to detect and discover potential defects by reporting classes that are similar (even not identical) to the detected defects. However, these approaches depend on the quality and the efficiency of data, i.e., defect instances, to learn from. Indeed, the high level of false positives represents the main obstacle for these approaches.

2.1.6 Visualization-Based Approaches

The high rate of false positives generated by the above-mentioned approaches encouraged other teams to explore semiautomated solutions. These solutions took the form of visualization-based environments. The primary goal is to take advantage of the human capability to integrate complex contextual information in the detection process. Kothari *et al.* [35] present a pattern-based framework for developing tool support to detect software anomalies by representing potential defects with different colors. Dhambri *et al.* [36] have proposed a visualization-based approach to detect design anomalies by automatically detecting some symptoms and letting others to human analyst. The visualization metaphor was chosen specifically to reduce the complexity of dealing with a large amount of data. Although visualization-based approaches are efficient to examine potential defects on their program and in their context, they do not scale to large systems easily. In addition, they require great human expertise and thus they are still time-consuming and error-prone strategies. Moreover, the information visualized is mainly metric based, meaning that complex relationships can be difficult to detect. Indeed, since visualization approaches and tools such as VERSO [37] are based on manual and human inspection, they still not only slow and time-consuming but also subjective.

Although these approaches have contributed significantly to automate the detection of design defects, none have presented a complete and fully automated technique. Detecting design defects is still, to some extent, a difficult, time-consuming, and manual process [38]. Indeed, the number of software defects typically exceeds the resources available to address them. In many cases, mature software projects are forced to ship with both known and unknown defects for lack of development resources to deal with every defect. Thus, to correct detected design defects and improve software quality the most useful and efficient software engineering activity is the refactoring.

2.2 Correction of Design Defects

2.2.1 Manual and Semiautomated Approaches

In Fowler's book [9], a nonexhaustive list of low-level design problems in source code have been defined. For each design problem (i.e., design defect), a particular list of possible refactorings are suggested to be applied by software maintainers manually. Indeed, in the literature, most of existing approaches are based on quality metrics improvement to deal with refactoring. In Ref. [21], Sahraoui et al. have proposed an approach to detect opportunities of code transformations (i.e., refactorings) based on the study of the correlation between some quality metrics and refactoring changes. To this end, different rules are defined as a combination of metrics/thresholds to be used as indicators for detecting bad smells and refactoring opportunities. For each bad smell, a predefined and standard list of transformations should be applied in order to improve the quality of the code. Another similar work is proposed by Du Bois et al. [19] who starts from the hypothesis that refactoring opportunities correspond to those which improves cohesion and coupling metrics to perform an optimal distribution of features over classes. Du Bois et al. analyze how refactorings manipulate coupling and cohesion metrics, and how to identify refactoring opportunities that improve these metrics. However, this two approaches are limited to only some possible refactoring operations with few number of quality metrics. In addition, the proposed refactoring strategies cannot be applied for the problem of correcting design defects.

Moha *et al.* [39] proposed an approach that suggests refactorings using formal concept analysis (FCA) to correct detected design defects. This work combines the efficiency of cohesion/coupling metrics with FCA to suggest refactoring opportunities. However, the link between defect detection and correction is not obvious, which makes the inspection difficult for the maintainers. Similarly, Joshi *et al.* [40] have presented a approach based on concept analysis aimed at identifying less cohesive classes. It also helps identify less cohesive methods, attributes, and classes in one go. Further, the approach guides refactoring opportunities identification such as extract class, move method, localize attributes, and remove unused attributes. In addition, Tahvildari *et al.* [6] also proposed a framework of object-oriented metrics used to suggest to the software engineer refactoring opportunities to improve the quality of an object-oriented legacy system.

Other contributions are based on rules that can be expressed as assertions (invariants, pre- and postcondition). The use of invariants has been proposed to detect parts of program that require refactoring by Kataoka *et al.* [41]. In addition, Opdyke [42] has proposed the definition and the use of pre- and postcondition with invariants to preserve the behavior of the software when applying refactoring. Hence, behavior preservation is based on the verification/satisfaction of a set of pre- and postcondition. All these conditions are expressed in terms of rules.

The major limitation of these manual and semiautomated approaches is that they try to apply refactorings separately without considering the whole program to be refactored and its impact on the other artifacts. Indeed, these approaches are limited to only some possible refactoring operations and few number of quality metrics to assess quality improvement. In addition, the proposed refactoring strategies cannot be applied for the problem of design defects correction. Another important issue is that these approaches do not take into consideration the effort needed to apply the suggested refactorings neither the semantic coherence of the refactored program.

Recently, there exist a few works focusing on refactorings that involve semantic preservation. Bavota *et al.* [17] have proposed an approach of automating the refactoring extract class based on graph theory that exploits structural and semantic relationships between methods. The proposed approach uses a weighted graph to represent the class to be refactored, where each node represents a method of that class. The weight of an edge that connects two nodes (representing methods) is a measure of the structural and semantic relationship between two methods that contribute to class cohesion. After that, they split the built graph in two subgraphs, to be used later to build two new classes having higher cohesion than the original class. In Ref. [43], Baar *et al.* have presented a simple criterion and a proof technique for the semantic preservation of refactoring rules that are defined for UML class diagrams and OCL constraints. Their approach is based on the formalization of the OCL semantics taking the form of graph transformation rules. However, their approach does not provide a concrete semantic preservation since there is no explicit differentiation between behavior and semantic preservation. In fact, they consider that the semantic preservation *means that the observable behaviors of original and refactored programs coincide.* However, they use the semantic preservation in the model level with a high level of abstraction and therefore the code level and the implementation issues are not considered. In addition, this approach uses only the refactoring move attribute and does not consider an exhaustive list of refactorings [12]. Another semantics-based framework has been proposed by Logozzo [44] for the definition and manipulation of class hierarchies-based refactorings. The framework is based on the notion of observable of a class, i.e., an abstraction of its semantics when focusing on a behavioral property of interest. They define a semantic subclass relation, capturing the fact that a subclass preserves the behavior of its superclass up to a given observed property.

The most limitation of the mentioned works is that the definition of semantic preservation is closely related to behavior preservation. Preserving the behavior does not means that the semantics of the refactored program is also preserved. Another issue is that the proposed techniques are limited to a small number of refactorings and thus it could not be generalized and adapted for an exhaustive list of refactorings. Indeed, the semantic preservation is still hard to ensure since the proposed approaches do not provide a pragmatic technique or an empirical study to prove whether the semantic coherence of the refactored program is preserved.

As far as semantic preservation issues, the above-mentioned approaches do not provide a fully automated framework for automating the refactoring task. Several studies have been focused on automating software refactoring in recent years using different meta-heuristic search-based techniques for automatically searching for the suitable refactorings to be applied.

2.2.2 Meta-Heuristic Search-Based Approaches

In this section, we summarize existing approaches where search-based techniques have been used to automate refactoring activities.

The majority of existing work combines several metrics in a single fitness function to find the best sequence of refactorings. Seng *et al.* [14] have proposed a single-objective optimization based-approach using GA [23] to suggest a list of refactorings to improve software quality. The search process uses a single fitness function to maximize a weighted sum of several quality metrics. The used metrics are mainly related to various class-level properties such as coupling, cohesion, complexity, and stability. Indeed, the authors have used some preconditions for each refactoring. These conditions serve at preserving the program behavior (refactoring feasibility). However, in this approach, the semantic coherence of the refactored program is not considered. In addition, the approach was limited only on the refactoring operation move method. Furthermore, there is the work of O'Keeffe *et al.* [20,63] that have used different local search-based techniques such as hill climbing and simulated annealing (SA) to provide an automated refactoring support. Eleven weighted object-oriented design metrics have been used to evaluate the quality improvements. In Ref. [16], Qayum *et al.* considered the problem of refactoring scheduling as a graph transformation problem. They expressed refactorings as a search for an optimal path, using Ant colony optimization, in the graph where nodes and edges represent, respectively, refactoring candidates and dependencies between them. However, the use of graphs is limited only on structural and syntactical information and therefore does not consider the domain semantics of the program neither its runtime behavior. Furthermore, Fatiregun *et al.* [15,45] have proposed another search-based approach for finding program transformations. They apply a number of simple atomic transformation rules called axioms. Indeed, the authors presume that if each axiom preserves semantics, then a whole sequence of axioms ought to preserve semantic equivalence. However, semantic equivalence depends on the program and the context, and therefore, it could not be always proved. Indeed, the semantic equivalence is based only on structural rules related to the axioms and no real semantic analysis has been performed. Recently, Otero *et al.* [46] use a new search-based refactoring. The core idea in this work is to explore the addition of a refactoring step into the genetic programming iteration. There will be an additional loop in which refactoring steps drawn from a catalog of such steps will be applied to individuals of the population. By adding in the refactoring step, the code evolved is simpler and more idiomatically structured, and therefore more readily understood and analyzed by human programmers than that produced by traditional GP methods.

Harman *et al.* [13] have proposed a search-based approach using Pareto optimality that combines two quality metrics, CBOs (coupling between objects) and SDMPC (standard deviation of methods per class), in two separate fitness functions. The authors start from the assumption that good design quality results from good distribution of features (methods) among classes. Their Pareto optimality-based algorithm succeeded in finding good sequence of move method refactorings that should provide the best compromise between CBO and SDMPC to improve code quality. However, one of the limitations of this approach is that it is limited to unique refactoring operation (move method) to improve software quality and only two metrics to evaluate the preformed improvements. In addition, it is odd that there is no semantic evaluator to prove that the semantic coherence is preserved.

To conclude, each approach has its strengths and weaknesses. It helps for conducting research for automating the detection and the correction (refactoring) of design defects. In Section 3, we describe our contributions and we show how to circumvent the above-mentioned problems in both detection and correction steps. Even though most of existing refactoring approaches are powerful, to some extent, to detect design defects and to provide refactoring solutions, as discussed above, several open issues need to be addressed.

3. PROPOSAL

In this section, we describe our proposal to circumvent the problems identified in the related work and mentioned in Section 1.2. Hence, we start by presenting our research objective addressed by our research work. We next give an overview of our methodology to achieve these goals.

3.1 Research Objective

The main objective of our research lies mainly in design defects detection and correction as a multiobjective search problem to find the compromise between the different objectives discussed in the previous section: improving the quality, preserving semantics, and reducing the effort. The aim is to circumvent the problems outlined in Section 1.2 using search-based software engineering techniques to automate the detection and correction of design defects.

3.2 Methodology

To achieve our research objectives and circumvent the above-mentioned issues in Section 1.2, we propose an approach in two steps:

1. Design defects detection: we consider the detection step as a search-based process to find the suitable detection rules for each type of design defect, by means of a GA [23]. We use real instance examples of design defects to derive detection rules.

2. Design defects correction: we use the derived detection rules to find the best refactoring solution, which maximizes the quality (by minimizing the number of detected defects). At the same time, we optimize other objectives such as minimizing the effort needed to apply refactorings, minimize semantic errors, and maximize similarity with good refactorings applied in the past to similar contexts.

Figure 4.1 gives an overview of our different contributions. The following subsections give more details about our expected contributions.

3.2.1 Step 1: Defects Detection

For the detection step, our proposal consists of using knowledge from previously manually inspected projects (called defects examples) in order to detect design defects that will serve to generate new detection rules based on combinations of quality metrics and threshold values. In short, the suitable detection rules are automatically derived by an optimization process based on GA [23] that exploits the available examples.

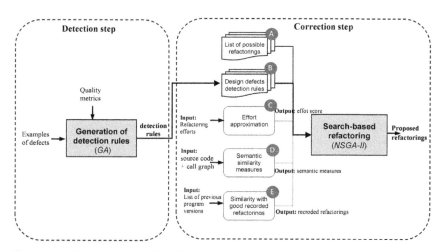

Figure 4.1 Our research methodology.

3.2.2 Step 2: Defects Correction

To correct the detected design defects, we use a search-based process to find the suitable refactoring solutions. To this end, use single-objective optimization-based approach driven by quality improvement. Then, we extend our approach by including different objectives as multiobjective optimization search-based process.

a. Quality-based refactoring suggestion

Our proposed approach aims at finding, from an exhaustive list of possible refactorings [12], the suitable refactoring solutions that fix the detected defects by means of a GA [23]. Hence, a refactoring solution corresponds to a sequence of refactoring operations that should minimize as much as possible the number of defects. To this end, our search-based process is guided by an evaluation function that calculates the number of detected design defects using learned detection rules from the step 1. Our approach takes as input a source code with defects and as output it suggests the suitable refactoring solutions.

b. Multiobjective refactoring suggestion

We extend this contribution starting from the observation that finding refactoring solutions based only on the quality criteria is not enough to obtain optimal refactoring solutions. In addition to the quality criterion, we explore other objectives to optimize. Thus, to improve our suggested refactoring solutions, a multiobjective search-based approach is also used. The process aims at finding the optimal sequence of refactoring operations that optimize the following objectives:

- Minimize the number of detected defects
- Minimize the number of code changes needed to apply refactorings
- Ensure the semantic preservation
- Maximize the similarity with refactorings applied in the past to similar contexts.

Thus, the number of changes corresponds to the code modification score and the cost of implementing the refactoring solution. This also includes understanding and addressing the impact of these operations. On the other hand, the semantic preservation insures that the refactored program is semantically equivalent to the original one, and that it models correctly the domain semantics. Indeed, we use knowledge from historical code changes to propose new refactoring solutions in similar contexts to improve the automation of refactoring.

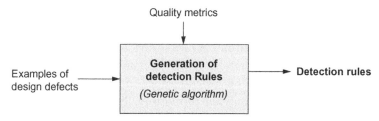

Figure 4.2 Overview of our design defects detection approach.

4. DESIGN DEFECTS DETECTION

In this section, we describe our proposal for the detection of design defects. To this end, knowledge from real defect examples is used to generate detection rules. As illustrated in Fig. 4.2, our approach takes as inputs a base (i.e., a set) of defect examples and a set of quality metrics (the definition and the usefulness of these metrics were defined and discussed in the literature [3]). As output, our approach derives a set of detection rules. Using GA, our rules derivation process generates randomly, from a given list of quality metrics, a combination of quality metrics/threshold for each defect type. Thus, the generation process can be viewed as a search-based combinatorial optimization to find the suitable combination of metrics/thresholds that best detect the defects examples. In other words, the best set of rules is the one that detects the maximum number of defects (we consider both precision and recall scores).

In the next subsection, we give an overview of GA and we describe its adaptation for the automatic generation of detection rules.

4.1 Genetic Algorithm Overview

GA is a powerful heuristic search optimization method inspired by the Darwinian theory of evolution [23]. The basic idea is to explore the search space by making a population of candidate solutions, also called individuals, evolve toward a "good" solution of a specific problem. In the GA, a solution is a (computer) program which is usually represented as a tree, where the internal nodes are functions, and the leaf nodes are terminal symbols. Both the function set and the terminal set must contain elements that are appropriate for the target problem. For instance, the function set can contain arithmetic operators, logic operators, mathematical functions, etc., whereas the terminal set can contain the variables (attributes) of the target problem. Every individual of the population is evaluated by a fitness function that determines a quantitative measure of its ability to solve the target problem. The exploration of the search space is achieved by the evolution of candidate solutions using selection and genetic operators such as crossover and mutation. The selection operator insures the selection of individuals in the current population proportionally to their fitness values so that the fitter an individual is, the higher the probability is that it be allowed to transmit its features to new individuals by undergoing crossover and/or mutation operators. The crossover operator insures the generation of new children, or offspring, based on parent individuals. The crossover operator allows transmission of the features of the best fitted parent individuals to new individuals. This is usually achieved by replacing a randomly selected subtree of one-parent individual with a randomly chosen subtree from another parent individual to obtain one child. A second child is obtained by inverting parents. Finally, the mutation operator is applied, with a probability which is usually inversely proportional to its fitness value, to modify some randomly selected nodes in a single individual. The mutation operator introduces diversity into the population and allows escaping from local solutions found during the search.

Once the selection, mutation, and crossover operators have been applied with given probabilities, the individuals in the newly created generation are evaluated using the fitness function. This process is repeated iteratively, until a stopping criterion is met. The criterion usually corresponds to a fixed number of generations. The result of GA (the best solution found) is the fittest individual produced along all generations.

4.2 Genetic Algorithm Adaptation

A high-level view of the GA approach to the defect detection problem is summarized in Algorithm 1. The algorithm takes as input a set of quality metrics and a set of defect examples that were manually detected in some systems and finds a solution that corresponds to the set of detection rules that best detect the defects in the base of examples.

Output:

best=_solution: detection rule

Lines 1–3 construct the initial GA population which is a set of individuals that define possible detection rules. The function rules(R, Defect_Type) returns an individual I by randomly combining a set of metrics/thresholds that correspond to a specific defect type, e.g., blob, SC, or FD. The function set_of(I) returns a set of individuals, i.e., detection

Algorithm: DefectDetection
Input:
Set of quality metrics
Set of defect examples
Process:
1. I:= rules(R, Defect_Type)
2. P:= set_of(I)
3. initial_population(P, Max_size)
4. repeat
5.   for all I in P do
6.   detected_defects := execute_rules(R, I)
7.   fitness(I) := compare(detected_defects, defect_examples)
8.   end for
9.   best_solution := best_fitness(I);
10. P := generate_new_population(P)
11. it:=it+1;
12. until it=max_it
13. return best_solution
Output:
best_solution: detection rule

Algorithm 1: High-level pseudo-code for GA adaptation to our problem

rules, that corresponds to a GA population. Lines 4–13 encode the main GA loop, which explores the search space and constructs new individuals by combining metrics within rules. During each iteration, we evaluate the quality of each individual in the population and save the individual having the best fitness (line 9). We generate a new population ($p + 1$) of individuals (line 10) by iteratively selecting pairs of parent individuals from population p and applying the crossover operator to them; each pair of parent individuals produces two children (new solutions). We include both the parent and child variants in the new population p. Then, we apply the mutation operator with a probability score for both parent and child to ensure the solution diversity; this produces the population for the next generation. The algorithm terminates when the termination criterion (maximum iteration number) is met and returns the best set of detection rules (best solution found during all iterations).

To adapt GA for a specific problem, the following elements have to be defined: representation of the individuals; creation of a population of individuals; definition of the fitness function to evaluate individuals for their ability to solve the problem under consideration; selection of the individuals to transmit from one generation to another; creation of new individuals using genetic operators (crossover and mutation) to explore the search space; and finally the generation of a new population.

4.2.1 Individual Representation

An individual is a set of IF–THEN rules. An example of the rule interpretation of an individual can be as follows:

R1: **IF** (LOCCLASS(c) $\geq$ 1500 AND LOCMETHOD(m,c) $\geq$ 129) OR (NMD(c) $\geq$ 100) **THEN** blob(c)

R2: **IF** (LOCMETHOD(m,c) $\geq$ 151) **THEN** spaghetti code(c)

R3: **IF** (NPRIVFIELD(c) $\geq$ 7 AND NMD(c) = 16) **THEN** functional decomposition (c)

Consequently, a detection rule has the following structure:

IF "Combination of metrics with their threshold values" THEN "Defect type"

The IF clause describes the conditions or situations under which a defect type is detected. These conditions correspond to logical expressions that combine some metrics and their threshold values using logic operators (AND, OR). If some of these conditions are satisfied by a class, then this class is detected as the defect figuring in the THEN clause of the rule. Consequently, THEN clauses highlight the defect types to be detected. We will have as many rules as types of defects to be detected. In our case, mainly for illustrative reasons, and without loss of generality, we focus on the detection of three defect types, namely blob, SC, and FD. Consequently, as shown in Fig. 4.3, we have three rules, R1 to detect blobs, R2 to detect SCs, and R3 to detect FD.

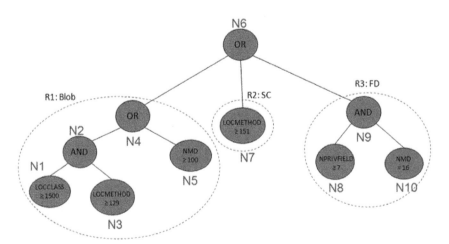

Figure 4.3 A tree representation of an individual.

One of the most suitable computer representations of rules is based on the use of trees [47]. In our case, the rule interpretation of an individual will be handled by a tree representation which is composed of two types of nodes: terminals and functions. The terminals (leaf nodes of a tree) correspond to different quality metrics with their threshold values. The functions that can be used between these metrics correspond to logical operators, which are Union (OR) and Intersection (AND).

Consequently, the rule interpretation of the individual of Fig. 4.3 has the following tree representation of Fig. 4.3. This tree representation corresponds to an OR composition of three subtrees, each subtree representing a rule: R1 OR R2 OR R3.

For instance, rule R1 is represented as a subtree of nodes starting at the branch (N1–N5) of the individual tree representation of Fig. 4.3. Since this rule is dedicated to detect blob defects, we know that the branch (N1–N5) of the tree will figure out the THEN clause of the rule. Consequently, there is no need to add the defect type as a node in the subtree dedicated to a rule.

4.2.2 Generation of an Initial Population

To generate an initial population, we start by defining the maximum tree length including the number of nodes and levels. The actual tree length will vary with the number of metrics to use for defect detection notice that a high tree length value does not necessarily mean that the results are more precise since, usually, only a few metrics are needed to detect a specific defect. These metrics can be either specified by the user or determined randomly. Because the individuals will evolve with different tree lengths (structures), with the root (head) of the trees unchanged, we randomly assign for each one:

- one metric and threshold value to each leaf node
- a logic operator (AND, OR) to each function node

Since any metric combination is possible and correct semantically, we do need to define some conditions to verify when generating an individual.

4.2.3 Selection and Genetic Operators

Selection To select the individuals that will undergo the crossover and mutation operators, we used stochastic universal sampling (SUS) [48], in which the probability to select an individual is directly proportional to its relative fitness in the population. For each iteration, we used SUS to select *population_size/2* individuals from population p to form population $p + 1$.

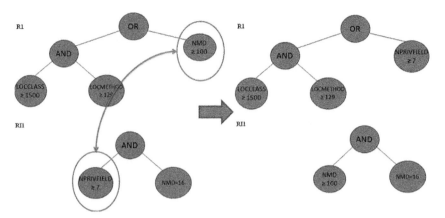

Figure 4.4 Crossover operator.

These (population_size/2) selected individuals will "give birth" to another (population_size/2) new individuals using crossover operator.

Crossover Two parent individuals are selected, and a subtree is picked on each one. Then, the crossover operator swaps the nodes and their relative subtrees from one parent to the other. The crossover operator can be applied only on parents having the same type of defect to detect. Each child thus combines information from both parents.

Figure 4.4 shows an example of the crossover process. In fact, the rule R1 and a rule RI1 from another individual (solution) are combined to generate two new rules. The right subtree of R1 is swapped with the left subtree of RI1.

As a result, after applying the cross operator, the new rule R1 to detect blob will be:

R1: **IF** (LOCCLASS(c) $\geq$ 1500 AND LOCMETHOD(m,c) $\geq$ 129)) OR (NPRIVFIELD(c) $\geq$ 7) **THEN** blob(c)

Mutation The mutation operator can be applied to either function or terminal nodes. This operator can modify one or many nodes. Given a selected individual, the mutation operator first randomly selects a node in the tree representation of the individual. Then, if the selected node is a terminal (threshold value of a quality metric), it is replaced by another terminal. The new terminal either corresponds to a threshold value of the same metric or the metric is changed and a threshold value is randomly fixed. If the selected node is a function (AND operator, for example), it is replaced by a new function (i.e., AND becomes OR). If a tree mutation is

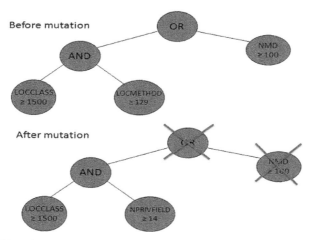

Figure 4.5 Mutation operator.

to be carried out, the node and its subtrees are replaced by a new randomly generated subtree.

To illustrate the mutation process, consider again the example that corresponds to a candidate rule to detect blob defects. Figure 4.5 illustrates the effect of a mutation that deletes the node NMD, leading to the automatic deletion of node OR (no left subtree), and that replaces the node LOCMETHOD by node NPRIVFIELD with a new threshold value. Thus, after applying the mutation operator, the new rule R1 to detect blob will be:

R1: IF (LOCCLASS(c) $\geq$ 1500 AND NPRIVFIELD(c) $\geq$ 14)) THEN
    blob(c)

4.2.4 Decoding of an Individual

The quality of an individual is proportional to the quality of the different detection rules composing it. In fact, the execution of these rules on the different projects extracted from the base of examples detects various classes as defects. Then, the quality of a solution (set of rules) is determined with respect to the number of detected defects in comparison to the expected ones in the base of examples. In other words, the best set of rules is the one that detects the maximum number of defects.

For instance, let us suppose that we have a base of defect examples having three classes X, W, and T that are considered, respectively, as blob, FD, and another blob. A solution contains different rules that detect only X as blob.

In this case, the quality of this solution will have a value of $1/3 = 0.33$ (only one detected defect over three expected ones).

4.2.5 Evaluation of an Individual

The encoding of an individual should be formalized in a fitness function that quantifies the quality of the generated rules. The goal is to define an efficient and simple (in the sense of not computationally expensive) fitness function in order to reduce computational complexity.

As discussed in Section 3.2.1, the fitness function aims to maximize the number of detected defects in comparison to the expected ones in the base of examples. In this context, we define the fitness function of a solution, normalized in the range [0, 1], as

$$f_{norm} = \frac{\frac{\sum_{i=1}^{p} a_i}{t} + \frac{\sum_{i=1}^{p} a_i}{p}}{2} \tag{4.1}$$

where t is the number of defects in the base of examples, p is the number of detected classes with defects, and a_i has value 1 if the ith detected class exists in the base of examples (with the same defect type), and value 0 otherwise.

To illustrate the fitness function, we consider a base of examples containing one system evaluated manually. In this system, six (6) classes are subject to three (4.1) types of defects as shown in Table 4.1.

The classes detected after executing the solution generating the rules R1, R2, and R3 of Fig. 4.3 are described in Table 4.2.

Table 4.1 Defects Example

Class	Blob	Functional Decomposition	Spaghetti Code
Student		X	
Person		X	
University		X	
Course	X		
Classroom			X
Administration	X		

Table 4.2 Detected Classes

Class	Blob	Functional Decompostion	Spaghetti Code
Person		X	
Classroom	X		
Professor		X	

Thus, only one class corresponds to a true defect (Person). Classroom is a defect, but the type is wrong and Professor is not a defect. The fitness function has the value:

$$f_{norm} = \frac{\frac{1}{3} + \frac{1}{6}}{2} = 0.25$$

with $t = 3$ (only one defect is detected over three expected defects), and $p = 6$ (only one class with a defect is detected over six expected classes with defects).

4.3 Validation

To test our approach, we studied its usefulness to guide quality assurance efforts for some open-source programs. In this section, we describe our experimental setup and present the results of an exploratory study.

4.3.1 Goals and Objectives

The goal of the study is to evaluate the efficiency of our approach for the detection and correction of maintainability defects from the perspective of a software maintainer conducting a quality audit. We present the results of the experiment aimed at answering the following research questions:

- **RQ1:** To what extent can the proposed approach detect maintainability defects?
- **RQ2:** What types of defects does it locate correctly?

To answer RQ1, we used an existing corpus of known design defects [7,25, 32,49] to evaluate the precision and recall of our approach. We compared our results to those produced by an existing rule-based strategy [7]. To answer RQ2, we investigated the type of defects that were found.

4.3.2 Systems Studied

We used six open-source Java projects to perform our experiments: GanttProject (Gantt for short) v1.10.2, Quick UML v2001, AZUREUS v2.3.0.6, LOG4J v1.2.1, ArgoUML v0.19.8, and Xerces-J v2.7.0. Table 4.3 provides some relevant information about the programs. The base of defect examples contains more than examples as presented in Table 4.3.

We chose the Xerces-J, ArgoUML, LOG4J, AZUREUS, Quick UML, and Gantt libraries because they are medium-sized open-source projects and were analyzed in related work. The version of Gantt studied was known to be of poor quality, which led to a major revised version. ArgoUML, Xerces-J, LOG4J, AZUREUS, and Quick UML, on the other hand, has

Table 4.3 Program Statistics

Systems	Number of Classes	KLOC	Number of Defects
GanttProject v1.10.2	245	31	41
Xerces-J v2.7.0	991	240	66
ArgoUML v0.19.8	1230	1160	89
Quick UML v2001	142	19	11
LOG4J v1.2.1	189	21	17
AZUREUS v2.3.0.6	1449	42	93

been actively evolved over the past 10 years, and their design has not been responsible for a slowdown of their developments.

In Ref. [7], Moha *et al.* asked three groups of students to analyze the libraries to tag instances of specific antipatterns to validate their detection technique, DECOR. For replication purposes, they provided a corpus of describing instances of different antipatterns that include blob classes, SC, and FDs. As described in Section 1, blobs are classes that do or know too much; SC is a code that does not use appropriate structuring mechanisms; finally, FD is a code that is structured as a series of function calls. These represent different types of design risks. In our study, we verified the capacity of our approach to locate classes that corresponded to instances of these antipatterns. We used a sixfold cross-validation procedure. For each fold, one open-source project is evaluated by using the remaining five systems as the base of examples. For example, Xerces-J is analyzed using detection rules generated from some defect examples from ArgoUML, LOG4J, AZUREUS, Quick UML, and Gantt.

The obtained results were compared to those of DECOR. Since Moha *et al.* [7] reported the number of antipatterns detected, the number of true positives, the recall (number of true positives over the number of maintainability defects), and the precision (ratio of true positives over the number detected), we determined the values of these indicators when using our algorithm for every antipattern in Xerces-J, AZUREUS, LOG4J, Quick UML, ArgoUML, and Gantt.

4.3.3 Comparative Results

Table 4.4 summarizes our findings. For Gantt, our average antipattern detection precision was 94%. DECOR, on the other hand, had a combined precision of 59% for the same antipatterns. The precision for Quick UML was about 86%, over twice the value of 43% obtained with DECOR. In particular, DECOR did not detect any SC in contradistinction with our approach. For Xerces-J, our precision average was 90%, while DECOR

Table 4.4 Detection Results

System	Precision (%)	Precision DECOR (%)	Recall (%)	Recall (%) DECOR (%)
GanttProject	Blob: 100	90	100	
	SC: 93	71.4	97	
	FD: 91	26.7	94	
Xerces-J	Blob: 97	88.6	100	
	SC: 90	60.5	88	
	FD: 88	51.7	86	
ArgoUML	Blob: 93	86.2	100	
	SC: 88	86.4	91	
	FD: 82	38.6	89	
QuickUML	Blob: 94	100	98	100
	SC: 84	0	93	
	FD: 81	30	88	
AZUREUS	Blob: 82	92.7	94	
	SC: 71	81.7	81	
	FD: 68	38.6	86	
LOG4J	Blob: 87	100	90	
	SC: 84	66.7	84	
	FD: 66	54.5	74	

had a precision of 67% for the same dataset. Finally, the comparison results were mixed for ArgoUML, AZUREUS, and LOG4J; still, our precision was consistently higher than 75% in comparison to DECOR.

On the negative side, our obtained recall score for the different systems was systematically less than that of DECOR. In fact, the rules defined in DECOR are large and this may explain the lower score in terms of precision. However, in such situations, DECOR has better results. The main reason that our approach finds better precision results is that the threshold values are well defined using our GA. Indeed, with DECOR, the user should test different threshold values to find the best ones. Thus, it is a fastidious task to find the best threshold combination for all metrics. The blob defect is detected better using DECOR because it is easy to find the thresholds and metrics combination for this kind of defects. The hypothesis to have 100% of recall justifies low precision, sometimes, to detect defects. In fact, there is a compromise between precision and recall. The detection of FDs by only using metrics seems difficult. This difficulty is alleviated in DECOR by including an analysis of naming conventions to perform the detection process. However, using naming conventions leads to results that depend on the coding practices of the development team. We obtained

Table 4.5 Detection Results

System	Precision GA (%)	Precision SA (%)
GanttProject	Blob: 100	100
	SC: 93	94
	FD: 91	90
Xerces-J	Blob: 97	83
	SC: 90	69
	FD: 88	79
ArgoUML	Blob: 93	80
	SC: 88	84
	FD: 82	67
QuickUML	Blob: 94	100
	SC: 84	88
	FD: 81	83
AZUREUS	Blob: 82	91
	SC: 71	63
	FD: 68	54
LOG4J	Blob: 87	100
	SC: 84	88
	FD: 66	73

comparable results without having to leverage lexical information. We can also mention that fixed defects correspond to the different defect types.

In the context of this experiment, we can conclude that our technique is able to identify design anomalies, in average, more accurately than DECOR (answer to research question RQ1 above).

As described in Table 4.5, we compared our GA detection results with those obtained by another local search algorithm, SA. The detection results for SA are also acceptable. For small systems, the precision when using SA is even better than with GA. In fact, GA is a global search that performs best in a large search space (which corresponds to large systems). In addition, the solution representation used in GA (tree) is suitable for rule generation, while SA uses a vector-based representation that is not. Furthermore, SA takes a lot of time, comparing to GA, to converge to an optimal solution (more than 10 min).

4.3.4 Discussion

We noticed that our technique does not have a bias toward the detection and correction of specific anomaly types. In Xerces-J, we had an almost equal distribution of each antipattern (14 SCs, 13 Blobs, and 14 FDs). On Gantt, the distribution was not as balanced, but this is principally due to the number of actual antipatterns in the system. We found all 4 known FDs

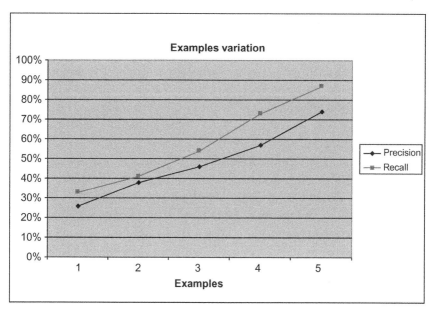

Figure 4.6 Examples-size variation (example = system).

and 9 Blobs in the system, and 8 of the 17 FDs, 4 more than DECOR. In Quick UML, we found 3 of 5 FDs; however, DECOR detected 3 of 10 FDs.

An important consideration is the impact of the example base size on detection quality. Drawn for AZUREUS, the results of Fig. 4.6 show that our approach also proposes good detection results in situations where only few examples are available. The precision and recall scores seem to grow steadily and linearly with the number of examples and rapidly grow to acceptable values (75%). Thus, our approach does not need a large number of examples to obtain good detection results.

The reliability of the proposed approach requires an example set of bad code. It can be argued that constituting such a set might require more work than identifying, specifying, and adapting rules. In our study, we showed that by using six open-source projects directly, without any adaptation, the technique can be used out of the box and will produce good detection precision and recall results for the detection of antipatterns for the studied systems.

In an industrial setting, we could expect that a company starts with some few open-source projects and gradually evolves its set of bad code examples to include context-specific data. This might be essential if we consider that different languages and software environments have different best/worst practices.

Finally, since we viewed the design defects detection problem as a combinatorial problem addressed with heuristic search, it is important to contrast the results with the execution time. We executed our algorithm on a standard desktop computer (Pentium CPU running at 2 GHz with 3 GB of RAM). The execution time for rules generation with a number of iterations (stopping criteria) fixed to 350 was less than 4 min (3 min 27 s) for both detection and correction. This indicates that our approach is reasonably scalable from the performance standpoint. However, the execution time depends on the number of used metrics and the size of the base of examples. It should be noted that more important execution times may be obtained than when using DECOR. In any case, our approach is meant to apply mainly in situations where manual rule-based solutions are not easily available.

5. DESIGN DEFECTS CORRECTION

In this section, we describe our approach for the design defects correction step. To correct the detected design defects, we propose a search-based approach that aims at finding, from an exhaustive list of possible refactorings [12], the suitable refactorings that fixe the detected defects. We show how we considered refactoring as a multiobjective optimization problem by integrating new objectives such as the code-changes minimization, semantic preservation, and similarity with recorded code changes.

5.1 Approach Overview

Our approach aims at exploring a huge search space to find refactoring solutions, i.e., sequence of refactoring operations, to correct bad smells. In fact, the search space is determined not only by the number of possible refactoring combinations but also by the order in which they are applied. Thus, a heuristic-based optimization method is used to generate refactoring solutions. We have four objectives to optimize: (1) maximize quality improvement (bad-smells correction), (2) minimize the number of semantic errors by preserving the way how code elements are semantically grouped and connected together, (3) minimize code changes needed to apply refactoring, and (4) maximize the consistency with development change history.

To this end, we consider the refactoring as a multiobjective optimization problem instead of a single-objective one using the NSGA-II [50].

Our approach takes as inputs a source code of the program to be refactored, a list of possible refactorings that can be applied, a set of bad-smells detection rules [21,24], our technique for approximating code changes needed to apply refactorings, a set of semantic measures, and a history of applied refactorings to previous versions of the system. Our approach generates as output the optimal sequence of refactorings, selected from an exhaustive list of possible refactorings, that improve the software quality by minimizing as much as possible the number of design defects, minimize code change needed to apply refactorings, preserve semantic coherence, and maximize the consistency with development change history.

In the following, we describe the formal formulation of our four objectives to optimize.

5.2 Modeling the Refactoring Process as a Multiobjective Problem

5.2.1 Quality

The quality criterion is evaluated using the fitness function given in Eq. (4.2). The quality value increases when the number of defects in the code is reduced after the correction. This function returns a real value between 0 and 1 that represents the proportion of defected classes (detected using bad-smells detection rules) compared to the total number of possible defects that can be detected. The detection of defects is based on some metrics-based rules defined in our previous work [21,24]:

$$Quality = \frac{\#corrected\,defects}{\#defects\,before\,applying\,refactorings} \tag{4.2}$$

5.2.2 Code Changes

Refactoring operations RO are classified into two categories: a low-level refactoring (LLR) or high-level refactoring (HLR) [21]. HLR is composed by the combination of two or more RO. However, LLR is an elementary and basic refactoring. The weight of each RO is an integer number, which belongs to the range $[1,3]$ depending on (1) code fragments complexity and (2) change impact. Formerly, the code changes score is defined as

$$Code\_change = \sum_{i=1}^{p} RO_i \tag{4.3}$$

Where p is the number of refactorings and RO_i is the weight of refactoring operations applied. More details can be found in our previous work [21].

5.2.3 Similarity with Recorded Code Changes

The overall idea is to maximize/encourage the use of new refactorings that are similar to those applied to same code fragments in the past. To calculate the similarity score between a proposed refactoring operation and different recorded/collected code changes, we use the following fitness function:

$$\text{Sim\_refactoring\_history } (RO_i) = \sum_{j=0}^{n-1} W * m \qquad (4.4)$$

where n is the size of the list of possible refactoring operations we use, m is the number of times that the same refactoring type has been applied in the past to the same code fragment/element, and w is a refactoring weight that calculates the similarities between refactoring types if an exact matching cannot be found with the base of recorded refactoring.

We consider two refactorings as similar if one of them is partially composed by the other or if their implementations are similar (using equivalent controlling parameters described in Table 4.6). Indeed, some complex refactorings such as extract class can be composed by move method, move field, create a new class, etc. In general, the weight w takes the values 2 if the refactoring is the same (for example, many move methods can be applied between the same source and target classes) or has similar implementation, 1 if one of the refactorings is compatible or composed partially by the other, otherwise 0 if the two refactorings are completely different. To calculate the similarity score of the whole proposed refactoring solution with historical code changes, we calculate the sum of the similarity value of each refactoring operation in this solution [26].

5.2.4 Semantic Preservation

Most of the refactorings are simple to implement and it is almost trivial to show that they preserve the behavior [9,42]. However, until now, there is no consensual way to investigate whether refactoring can preserve semantic coherence of the original program. To this end, we formulate semantic preservation using a metamodel to describe its related concepts from the perspective of automating the refactoring task. Furthermore, the aim is to provide a terminology around the refactoring to be used in this paper and also to be used by all the stakeholders. Figure 4.7 represents our metamodel.

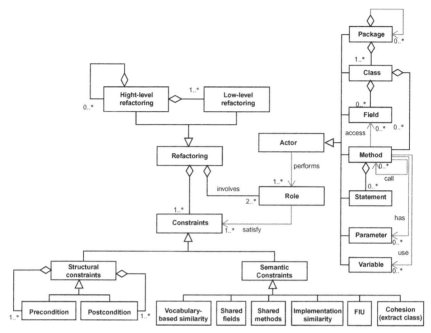

Figure 4.7 Refactoring metamodel.

Figure 4.7 describes our semantic-based refactoring metamodel. The class *refactoring* represents the main entity in our metamodel. As mentioned before, we classify refactoring operations into two categories: low- and high-level refactorings. A *low-level refactoring* is an elementary/basic program transformation for adding, removing, and renaming program elements (e.g., add method, remove field, and add relationship). These low-level refactorings can be combined to perform more complex refactorings called *high-level refactorings* (e.g., move method and extract class). Furthermore, a *high-level refactoring* is composed by one or many low- and/or high-level refactorings; for example, to perform extract class, we need to create a new empty class and apply a set of move methods and move fields.

To apply a refactoring operation, we need to specify which *actors*, i.e., code fragments, are involved/impacted by this refactoring and which *roles* they play to perform the refactoring operation. As illustrated in Fig. 4.7, an *actor* can be a *package*, *class*, *field*, *method*, *parameter*, *statement*, or *variable*. In Table 4.6, we specify for each refactoring its involved actors and their roles.

The class *constraints* consists of checking a set of constraints to satisfy the correctness of applied refactoring. Hence, we distinguish between two kinds of constrains: (1) *structural constraints* and (2) *semantic constraints*. The

Table 4.6 Refactoting Examples and Their Involved Actors and Roles

Ref	Refactorings	Actors	Roles
MM	Move method	Class	Source class, target class
		Method	Moved method
MF	Move field	Class	Source class, target class
		Field	Moved field
PUF	Pull-up field	Class	Subclasses, superclass
		Field	Moved field
PUM	Pull-up method	Class	Subclasses, superclass
		Method	Moved method
PDF	Push-down field	Class	Superclass, subclasses
		Field	Moved field
PDM	Push-down method	Class	Superclass, subclasses
		Method	Method
IC	Inline class	Class	Source class, target class
		Class	Source class, target class
EM	Extract method	Method	Source method, new method
		Statement	Moved statements
EC	Extract class	Class	Source class, new class
		Field	Moved fields
		Method	Moved methods
MC	Move class	Package	Source package, target package
		Class	Moved class
EI	Extract interface	Class	Source classes, new interface
		Field	Moved fields
		Method	Moved methods

structural constraints are extensively investigated in the literature. Opdyke defined, in Ref. [42], a set of pre- and postconditions for a large list of refactoring operations to ensure the structural consistence. Moreover, developers should exanimate manually all actors related to the refactoring to inspect the semantic relationship between them.

Vocabulary-based similarity (VS) This heuristic could be interesting to consider when moving methods, fields, methods, classes, etc. For example, when a method has to be moved from one class to another, the refactoring would probably make sense if both actors (source class and target class) share the same vocabulary [25]. Thus, the vocabulary could be used as an indicator of the semantic similarity between different actors that are involved by refactoring.

In the literature, the common idea of the refactoring is to redistribute/reorganize software elements, e.g., classes, methods, and variables, in order to improve software quality while preserving its behavior. However, this is not enough to give concrete vision of the refactoring. There is no formal framework for refactoring that involves the semantic issues and the effort needed for the code adaptation. Hence, it is extremely challenging to formalize refactoring involving these two concepts: the semantic validity and the effort. To this end, as a first step, we define a metamodel formalizing most of the refactoring concepts. Then, we show how we use these concepts to automatically suggest refactoring solutions to correct design defects in real systems.

We start from the assumption that the vocabulary of an actor is borrowed from the domain terminology and therefore could be used to determine which part of the domain semantics is encoded by an actor. Thus, two actors could be semantically similar if they use a similar/common vocabulary.

The vocabulary could be extracted from identifiers/names of methods, fields, variables, parameters, type declaration, etc. Then, we tokenize them using the Camel Case Splitter [51], one of the most used techniques in Software Maintenance tools for the preprocessing of identifiers. More pertinent vocabulary can be also extracted from comments, commits information, and documentation. Then, we calculate the percentage of common tokens/vocabulary using information retrieval-based techniques (e.g., cosine similarity). Equation (4.5) calculates cosine similarity between two actors using term frequency. Each actor is represented as a vocabulary vector, and each vector dimension is a term. The distance between two vectors is considered as an indicator of its similarity. Therefore, using cosine similarity, the conceptual similarity among a pair of actors c_1 and c_2 is quantified by

$$Sim(c_1, c_2) = \frac{\sum_{i=0}^{n-1} \left(tf_{c_1}(w_i) * tf_{c_2}(w_i) \right)}{\sqrt{\sum_{i=0}^{n-1} \left(tf_{c_1}(w_i) \right)^2} \sqrt{\sum_{i=0}^{n-1} \left(tf_{c_2}(wi) \right)^2}} \in [0, 1] \qquad (4.5)$$

where $tf_{c1}(w_i)$ and $tf_{c2}(w_i)$ are term frequency values of the term w_i in the representative vectors of actors $c1$ and $c2$.

Dependency-based similarity (DS) We approximate domain semantic closeness between actors starting from their mutual dependencies. The intuition is that actors that are strongly connected (i.e., having dependency links) are semantically related. As a consequence, refactoring operation requiring semantic closeness between involved actors is likely to be successful when these actors are strongly connected. In our measures, we consider two types of dependency links:

1. *Shared method call* that can be captured from call graph derived from the whole program using class hierarchy analysis [52]. A call graph is a directed graph which represents the different calls (call-in and call-out) among all methods of the entire program, in which nodes represent methods and edges represent calls between these methods. Then, for a pair of actors, shared calls are captured through this graph by identifying shared neighbors of nodes related to each actor. We consider both shared call-out and shared call-in. Equations (4.6) and (4.7) are used to measure, respectively, the shared call-out and the shared call-in between two actors c_1 and c_2 (two classes, for example).

$$\text{shared call out } (c_1, c_2) = \frac{2 \times |\text{call-out}(c_1) \cap \text{call-out}(c2)|}{|\text{call-out}(c_1) \cup \text{call-out}(c_2)|} \in [0, 1] \quad (4.6)$$

$$\text{shared call-in } (c_1, c_2) = \frac{2 \times |\text{call-in }(c_1) \cap \text{call-in }(c_2)|}{|\text{call-in}(c_1) \cup \text{call-in}(c_2)|} \in [0, 1] \quad (4.7)$$

A shared method call is defined as the average of shared call-in and call-out.

2. *Shared field access* that can be calculated by capturing all field references that occur using static analysis to identify dependencies based on field accesses (read or modify). We assume that two software elements are semantically related if they read or modify the same fields. The rate of shared fields (read or modified) between two actors c_1 and c_2 is calculated according to Eq. (4.5). In this equation, *fieldRW(c_i)* computes the number of fields that may be read or modified by each method of the actor c_i. Thus, by applying a suitable static program analysis to the whole method body, all field references that occur could be easily captured.

$$\text{shared field} \times RW(c_1, c_2) = \frac{2 \times |fieldRW(c_1) \cap fieldRW(c_2)|}{|fieldRW(c_1) \cup fieldRW(c_2)|} \in [0, 1] \quad (4.8)$$

Implementation-based similarity (IS) For some refactorings like pull-up method, methods with identical results on subclasses should be moved to its superclass [9]. Here the idea is to compare the implementation similarity between methods in subclasses in two levels: signature level and body level. To compare methods signatures, semantic comparison algorithm is applied to ensure that these methods have identical/similar signatures (names, parameter list, and return types). Let *Sig(m)* to be the set contains method name, parameters list, and return types. The signature similarity between two methods m_1 and m_2 is computed by comparing $Sig(m_1)$ to $Sig(m_2)$ as:

$$Sig\_Sim(m_1, m_2) = \frac{2 \times |Sim(m_1) \cap Sim(m_2)|}{|Sim(m_1) \cup Sim(m_2)|} \in [0, 1] \qquad (4.9)$$

Then to compare method bodies, we use Soot [52], a java optimization framework, to rapidly retrieve and then compare the number of statements which constitute the body, used local variables, exceptions handled in the body, call-out, and field references. Let $Body(m)$ to be the set of statements, local variables, exceptions, call-out, and field references of the method m. The body similarity of two methods m_1 and m_2 is computed by comparing $Body(m_1)$ to $Body(m_2)$ as:

$$Body\_Sim(m_1, m_2) = \frac{2 \times |Body(m_1) \cap Body(m_2)|}{|Body(m_1) \cup Body(m_2)|} \in [0, 1] \qquad (4.10)$$

The implementation similarity between two methods is computed as the average of their Sig_Sim and $Body\_Sim$ values.

Feature inheritance usefulness (FIU) This heuristic can be useful particularly when applying push-down method/field. In general, when a feature (method or field) is used by only few subclasses, then it is relevant to move it (i.e., push down it) to its subclasses [9]. To this end, we need to assess the usefulness of a method in their subclasses using a precise call graph in terms of polymorphic calls derived using RTA (Rapid Type Analysis) or VTA (Variable Type Analysis). The inheritance usefulness of a method is given by (4.11)

$$\text{FIU}(m, c) = \frac{\sum_{j=0}^{n-1} \text{call(m,i)}}{n} \in [0, 1] \qquad (4.11)$$

where n is the number of subclasses, m is the method to be moved from the class c, call is a function that return 1 if m is called in the subclass i, 0 otherwise.

Similarly, for push-down field, a suitable field reference analysis is used. The inheritance usefulness of a field is given by (4.12):

$$\text{FIU}(f, c) = \frac{\sum_{j=0}^{n-1} \text{Use}(f, c_i)}{n} \in [0, 1] \qquad (4.12)$$

where n is the number of subclasses, f is the field to be moved from the class c, use is a function that return 1 if f is used (read or modify) from the subclass c_i, 0 otherwise.

Cohesion-based dependency We use cohesion-based dependency (CD) measure especially for extract class refactoring. Hence, a new class can be extracted from a source class by moving a set of strongly related (cohesive) set of fields and methods from the original class into the new one. The best set improves the cohesion of the original class and minimizes the coupling with the new class. To this end, we study the CD in order to find a set of methods and fields that satisfy these criteria. In fact, when applying the extract class refactoring on a specific class, it will be splitted into two classes. Thus, we need to calculate the semantic similarity between elements in the original class to decide how to split it into two classes.

We use vocabulary-based similarity and dependency-based similarity to find this cohesive set of actors (methods and fields). Let us consider a source class that contains n methods $\{m_1, \ldots . m_n\}$ and m fields $\{f_1, \ldots . f_m\}$. The idea is to calculate the similarity between each element method–field and method–method in a matrix as shown in Table 4.7.

The cohesion matrix would be calculated as follows: for the similarity between method–method, we consider both vocabulary- and dependency-based similarity measurements. However, for the similarity method–field, we use only the second measure related to shared field, i.e., if the method m_i may access (read or write) to the field f_j, then the similarity value is 1 and 0 otherwise. The column average contains the average of similarity values for each line. Thus, the suitable set of methods and fields to be moved to the new class corresponds to the line which has a higher average value (i.e., the bold values in Table 4.7). Hence, the elements that should be moved are those which have a similarity value higher than a threshold value of 0.5.

5.3 NSGA-II for Software Refactoring

This section is dedicated to describe how we encoded the refactoring as a multiobjective optimization problem using the NSGA-II [50].

Table 4.7 An Example of Cohesion Matrix

	f_1	f_2	...	f_m	m_1	m_2	...	m_n	Average
m_1	1	0		1	1	0.15		0.1	0.42
m_2	**0**	**1**		**1**	**1**	**1**		**0**	**0.6**
· · ·									
m_n	1	0		0	0.6	0.2		1	0.32

5.3.1 NSGA-II Overview

The basic idea of NSGA-II [50] is to make a population of candidate solutions evolve toward the near-optimal solution in order to solve a multiobjective optimization problem. NSGA-II is designed to find a set of optimal solutions, called nondominated solutions, also Pareto set. A nondominated solution is the one which provides a suitable compromise between all objectives without degrading any of them. As described in Algorithm 2, the first step in NSGA-II is to create randomly a population P_0 of individuals encoded using a specific representation. Then, a child population Q_0 is generated from the population of parents P_0 using genetic operators such as crossover and mutation. Both populations are merged into an initial population R_0 of size N, and a subset of individuals is selected, based on the dominance principle and crowding distance [50] to create the next generation. This process will be repeated until reaching the last iteration according to stop criteria.

1. **while** *stopping criteria not reached* **do**
2. $R_t = P_t \cup Q_t$;
3. F = fast-non-dominated-sort (R_t);
4. $P_{t+1} = \emptyset$ and $i=1$;
5.   **while** $| P_{t+1}| + |F_i| \leq N$ **do**
6.   Apply crowding-distance-assignment(F_i);
7. $P_{t+1} = P_{t+1} \cup F_i$;
8. $i = i+1$;
9.   **end**
10.   Sort($F_i, \prec n$);
11. $P_{t+1} = P_{t+1} \cup F_i[1 : (N - | P_{t+1} |)]$;
12. Q_{t+1} = create-new-pop(P_{t+1});
13. $t = t+1$;
14. **end**

Algorithm 2: High-level pseudo-code for GA adaptation to our problem

5.3.2 NSGA-II Adaptation

This section describes how NSGA-II [50] can be used to find refactoring solutions with multiple conflicting objectives. To be applied, NSGA-II needs to specify some elements for its implementation: (1) the representation of individuals used to create a population; (2) a fitness function to evaluate the candidate solutions according to each objective; (3) the crossover and mutation operators that have to be designed according to the individual's representation. In addition, a method to select the best individuals has to be implemented to create the next generation of individuals. As output, NSGA-II returns the best individuals (with highest fitness scores) to explain the adaptation of the design of these elements for the generation of refactoring solutions using NSGA-II.

Solution Representation To represent a candidate solution (individual), we used a vector representation. Each vector's dimension represents a refactoring operation. When created, the order of applying these refactorings corresponds to their positions in the vector. For each of these refactorings, we specify pre- and postconditions that are already studied in Ref. [9] to ensure the feasibility of applying them. In addition, for each refactoring, a set of controlling parameters, e.g., actors and roles, as illustrated in Table 4.6, are randomly picked from the program to be refactored. An example of a solution is given in Fig. 4.8. For short, we use abbreviations, e.g., MM for move method refactoring and EC for extract class (see Table 4.6).

Fitness Functions After creating a solution, it should be evaluated using fitness function to ensure its ability to solve the problem under consideration. Since we have four objectives to optimize, we are using four different fitness functions to include in our NSGA-II adaptation. We used the four fitness functions that are described in the previous section:

1. *Quality fitness function* that calculates the ratio of the number of corrected design defects (bad smells) over the initial number of defects using detection rules [24].
2. *Semantic fitness function* that corresponds to the weighted sum of different semantic measures/heuristics described in Section 3. Hence, the semantic fitness function of a refactoring solution corresponds to the average of the semantic measure for each refactoring operation in the vector. In Table 4.8, we specify for each refactoring operation which measures/heuristics are combined to ensure its semantic coherence.
3. *Code changes fitness function* that approximates the amount of code changes needed to apply the suggested refactoring operations. To this end, we use the model described in Section 3.
4. *History of changes fitness function* that maximize/encourage the use of new refactorings that are similar to those applied to same code fragments in the past. To calculate the similarity score between a proposed refactoring operation and different recorded/collected code changes, we use the fitness function described in Section 3.

MM	MF	PUF	IM	EC	MF

Figure 4.8 Representation of an NSGA-II individual.

Table 4.8 Refactoring Operations and Its Semantic Heuristics

Refactorings	VS	DS	IS	FIU	CD
Move method	x	x			
Move field	x	x			
Pull-up field	x	x		x	
Pull-up method	x	x	x		
Push-down field	x	x		x	
Push-down method	x	x		x	
Inline class	x	x			
Extract class	x	x			x
Move class	x	x			
Extract interface	x	x			x

Selection To guide the selection process, NSGA-II sorts the population using the dominance principle and uses a comparison operator based on a calculation of the crowding distance [50] to select potential individuals to construct a new population $Pt + 1$. Then, to generate an offspring population $Qt + 1$, the selection of individuals that will undergo the crossover and mutation operators in our adaption of NSGA-II is based on the SUS algorithm [48].

Genetic Operators To better explore the search space, the crossover and mutation operators are defined. For crossover, we use a single, random, and cut-point crossover. It starts by selecting and splitting at random two parent solutions. Then, crossover creates two child solutions by putting, for the first child, the first part of the first parent with the second part of the second parent, and, for the second child, the first part of the second parent with the second part of the first parent. This operator must ensure the respect of the length limits by eliminating randomly some refactoring operations. As illustrated in Fig. 4.9, each child combines some of the refactoring operations of a parent with some ones of the second parent. In any given generation, each solution will be the parent in at most one crossover operation.

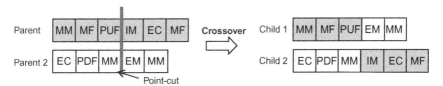

Figure 4.9 Crossover operator.

Figure 4.10 Mutation operator.

Mutation operator picks at random one or more operations from its associated sequence and replaces them by other ones from the initial list possible refactorings. An example is shown in Fig. 4.10.

5.4 Validation

To evaluate the efficiency of our approach for generating good refactorings, we conducted experiments based on six large open-source systems to answer our two research questions described in Section 1. We start by describing the designed our experiments. Then, we describe and discuss the obtained results.

To evaluate the efficiency of our approach for generating good refactorings, we conducted experiments based on two large open-source systems. We start by presenting our research questions. Then, we describe and discuss the obtained results.

5.4.1 Research Questions

In our study, we assess the performance of our refactoring proposal by finding out whether it could generate meaningful sequences of refactorings that fix design defects while reducing the number of code modification/change score, preserve the semantic coherence of the design, and reuse as much as possible a base of recorded code changes applied in the past to similar contexts. Indeed, our study aims at addressing six research questions, which are defined below. We also explain how our experiments are designed to address them. The six research questions are as follows:

RQ1: To what extent can the proposed approach correct design defects?

RQ2: To what extent can the proposed approach minimizes code changes while fixing defects?

RQ3: To what extent the proposed approach preserves the semantics when fixing defects?

RQ4: To what extent the use of recorded changes improve the suggestion of good refactoring and semantic coherence with similar correction rate?

RQ5: To what extent the use of multiple objectives is efficient for providing "good" refactoring suggestion strategies.

RQ6: How does the proposed multiobjective approach based on NSGA-II perform compared to other multiobjective algorithms or a mono-objective approach?

To answer **RQ1**, we validate manually the proposed refactoring operations to fix design defects. To this end, we calculate the defect correction ratio (DCR) given by Eq. (4.13). It corresponds to the number of defects that are corrected after applying the suggested refactoring solution.

$$DCR = \frac{\#corrected\,defects}{\#defects\,before\,applying\,refactorings} \in [0,1] \qquad (4.13)$$

To answer **RQ2**, we validated if the proposed refactorings are useful to fix detected defects with low code change scores. To this end, we calculate the code change reduction score. Code changes score is calculated using our model described in Section 5.2.2.

To answer **RQ3**, we manually inspect the semantic correctness of the proposed refactoring operations for each studied system. We applied the proposed refactoring operations using ECLIPSE [53], and we check the semantic coherence of the modified code fragments. To this end, we define the metric refactoring precision (RP) that corresponds to the number of meaningful refactoring operations, in terms of semantic coherence, over the total number of suggested ones. RP is given by Eq. (4.14).

$$RP = \frac{\#coherent\,refactorings}{\#proposed\,refactorings} \in [0,1] \qquad (4.14)$$

To answer **RQ4**, we use the metric RP to evaluate the effect of the use of recorded refactorings, applied in the past to similar contexts, on the semantic coherence. Moreover, in order to evaluate the importance of reusing collected refactorings in similar contexts, we define the metric, reused refactoring (RR) that calculates the percentage of operations from the base of collected changes (refactorings) used to generate the optimal refactoring solution by our proposal. RR is given by Eq. (4.15).

$$RR = \frac{\#used\,refactorings\,in\,the\,base\,of\,collected\,refactorings}{\#refactorings\,in\,the\,base\,of\,collected\,refactorings} \in [0,1]$$

$$(4.15)$$

For **RQ5**, we want to investigate the importance and the efficiency of using each objective to suggest optimal refactoring solutions and how our four objectives are useful. In addition, we want to ensure the usefulness of combining our four objectives together to provide near-optimal refactoring strategies. Thus, we compare the results of using only the quality improvement objective (defects correction) with different combinations of other objectives in terms of DCR, RP, and code change reduction. Moreover, we compare our approach to two other existing approaches: Kessentini et al. [24] and Harman et al. [13] that consider the refactoring suggestion task only from the quality improvement standpoint, other objectives are not considered.

Finally, to answer **RQ6**, we assessed the performance of the multiobjective algorithm NSGA-II compared to another multiobjective algorithm MOGA (Multiobjective Genetic Algorithm), a random search, and a GA where one fitness function is used (an average of the four objective scores).

5.4.2 Setup

We designed our experiments to address the above-mentioned research questions. To this end, we used a set of well-known and well-commented open-source java projects. We applied our approach to six large and medium size open-source java projects: Xerces-J [54], JFreeChart [55], GanttProject [56], AntApache [57], JHotDraw [58], and Rhino [59]. Xerces-J is a family of software packages for parsing XML. JFreeChart is a powerful and flexible Java library for generating charts. GanttProject is a cross-platform tool for project scheduling. AntApache is a build tool and library specifically conceived for Java applications. JHotDraw is a GUI framework for drawing editors. Finally, Rhino is a JavaScript interpreter and compiler written in Java and developed for the Mozilla/Firefox browser. We selected these systems for our validation because they range from medium- to large-sized open-source projects, which have been actively developed over the past 10 years, and their design has not been responsible for a slowdown of their developments. Table 4.9 provides some descriptive statistics about these six programs.

To collect refactorings applied in the previous program versions, and the expected refactorings applied to the next version of studied systems, we use Ref-Finder [60]. Ref-Finder, implemented as an Eclipse plug-in, can identify refactoring operations between two releases of a software system. Table 4.10 reports the analyzed versions and the number of refactoring operations, identified by Ref-Finder, between each subsequent couple of

Table 4.9 Program Statistics

Systems	Release	# Classes	# Defects	KLOC
Xerces-J	v2.7.0	991	66	240
JFreeChart	v1.0.9	521	57	170
GanttProject	v1.10.2	245	41	41
AntApache	v1.8.2	1191	82	255
JHotDraw	v6.1	585	21	21
Rhino	v1.7R1	305	61	42

Table 4.10 Analyzed Versions and Refactorings Collection

Systems	Expected Refactorings		Collected Refactorings	
	Next Release	# Refactorings	Previous Releases	# Refactorings
Xerces-J	v2.8.1	39	v1.4.2–2.6.1	70
JFreeChart	v1.0.11	31	v1.0.6–1.0.9	76
GanttProject	v1.11.2	46	v1.7–1.10.2	91
AntApache	v1.8.4	78	v1.2–1.8.2	247
JHotDraw	v6.2	27	v5.1–6.1	64
Rhino	1.7R4	46	v1.4R3–1.7R1	124

analyzed versions, after the manual validation. In our study, we consider only refactoring types described in Table 4.6.

The number of refactoring solutions to evaluate depends on different objectives' combinations: quality improvement Q, semantic preservation S, code change minimization CC, and recorded refactorings reuse RR. For each combination (two, three, or four objectives), a refactoring solution is suggested to find the best compromise between the considered objectives. Similarly, two refactoring solutions of both state-of-the-art works [13,24] are manually evaluated in order to compare them to our approach in terms of semantic coherence. Moreover, we have three multiobjective algorithms to be tested for refactoring suggestion task: NSGA-II [50], MOGA [61], and RS (random search) [62]. Table 4.11 describes the number of refactoring solutions to be evaluated for each studied system in order to answer our research questions.

As shown in Table 4.11, for each system, 18 refactoring solutions have to be evaluated. Due to the large number of refactoring operations to be evaluated (108 solutions in total, each solution consists of a set of refactoring

Table 4.11 Refactoring Solutions for Each Studied System

Ref. Solution	Algorithm/Approach	# Fitness Functions	Objectives Considered
Solution 1		2	Q, CC
Solution 2		2	Q, S
Solution 3	NSGA-II	3	Q, S, CC
Solution 4		3	Q, S, RR
Solution 5		4	Q, S, CC, RR
Solution 6		2	Q, CC
Solution 7		2	Q, S
Solution 8	MOGA	3	Q, S, CC
Solution 9		3	Q, S, RR
Solution 10		4	Q, S, CC, RR
Solution 11		2	Q, CC
Solution 12		2	Q , S
Solution 13	Random search (RS)	3	Q, S, CC
Solution 14		3	Q, S, RR
Solution 15		4	Q, S, CC, RR
Solution 16	Genetic algorithm	1	Q + S + CC + RR
Solution 17	Kessentini et al. [24]	1	Q
Solution 18	Harman et al. [13]	2	CBO, SDMPC

operations), we pick at random a subset of 10 refactorings per solution to be evaluated in our study.

Moreover, due to the stochastic nature of the algorithms/approaches we are studying, each time we execute an algorithm and we can get slightly different results. To cater for this issue and to make inferential statistical claims, our experimental study is performed based on 31 independent simulation runs for each algorithm/technique studied. Wolcoxon rank sum test is applied between NSGA-II and each of the other algorithms/techniques (Kessentini et al., Ouni et al., MOGA, and RS) in terms of DCR with a 99% confidence level ($\alpha = 1\%$). Our tests show that the obtained results are statistically significant with p-value<0.01 and not due to chance.

5.4.3 Algorithms Configuration
In our experiments, we use and compare different mono- and multiobjective algorithms. For each algorithm, to generate an initial population, we start by defining the maximum vector length (maximum number of operations per solution). The vector length is proportional to the number of refactorings that are considered and the size of the program to be refactored. A higher number of operations in a solution does not necessarily mean that

the results will be better. Ideally, a small number of operations should be sufficient to provide a good trade-off between the fitness functions. This parameter can be specified by the user or derived randomly from the sizes of the program and the used refactoring list. During the creation, the solutions have random sizes inside the allowed range. For all algorithms NSGA-II, MOGA, Random search, and GA, we fixed the maximum vector length to 700 refactorings, the population size to 200 individuals (refactoring solutions), and the maximum number of iterations to 6000 iterations. We also designed our NSGA-II adaptation to be flexible in a way that we can configure the number objectives and which objectives to consider in the execution.

5.4.4 Results

This section reports the results of our empirical study, which are further discussed in the next section. We first start by comparing our multiobjective approach using NSGA-II with two state-of-the-art techniques Harman *et al.* [13] and Kessentini *et al.* [24].

Table 4.12 summarizes our findings. To evaluate the efficiency of our approach, we compared our results to those produced by two existing contributions Harman *et al.* [13] and Kessentini *et al.* [24]. In Ref. [13], Harman *et al.* proposed a multiobjective approach that uses two quality metrics to improve (CBOs and SDMPC) after applying the refactorings sequence. In Ref. [24], a single-objective GA is used to correct defects by finding the best refactoring sequence that reduces the number of defects. The comparison is performed through three levels: (1) DCR that is calculated using defect detection, (2) RP that represents the results of the subject judgments, and (3) code changes needed to apply the suggested refactorings. We adapted our technique for calculating code changes' scores for both approaches Harman *et al.* and Kessentini *et al.*

As described in Table 4.12, the majority of suggested refactorings improve significantly the code quality with lower code changes while preserving the semantic coherence much better than two other approaches. On average, for all of our six studied systems, 80% of proposed refactoring operations are semantically feasible and do not generate semantic incoherence. This score is higher than the one of the other approaches having, respectively, only 36% and 35% as RP scores. Thus, our multiobjective approach reduces the number of semantic incoherencies when applying refactoring operations. Moreover, our approach succeeded in suggesting

Table 4.12 Empirical Study Results

Systems	Approach	DCR	RP	Changes' Score	RP Automatic
Xerces	NSGA-II	83% (55/66)	80 %	3369	23% (9/39)
	Harman *et al.* [13]	N.A	40 %	2669	8 % (3/39)
	Kessentini *et al.* [24]	89% (59/66)	37 %	4873	13% (5/39)
JFreeChart	NSGA-II	86% (49/57)	83 %	1979	35% (11/31)
	Harman *et al.* [13]	N.A	37 %	3269	0 % (0/31)
	Kessentini *et al.* [24]	91% (52/57)	37 %	3158	13% (4/31)
GanttProject	NSGA-II	85% (35/41)	80 %	2640	43% (20/46)
	Harman *et al.* [13]	N.A	23 %	4790	0% (0/46)
	Kessentini *et al.* [24]	95% (39/41)	27 %	4158	15% (7/46)
AntApache	NSGA-II	78% (64/82)	77 %	4458	31% (24/78)
	Harman *et al.* [13]	N.A	40 %	6987	04% (3/78)
	Kessentini *et al.* [24]	80% (66/82)	30 %	6587	0% (0/78)
JHotDraw	NSGA-II	86% (18/21)	80 %	2158	44% (18/41)
	Harman *et al.* [13]	N.A	37 %	3654	10% (4/41)
	Kessentini *et al.* [24]	90% (19/21)	43 %	3798	7% (3/41)
Rhino	NSGA-II	85% (52/61)	80 %	1698	35% (16/46)
	Harman *et al.* [13]	N.A	37 %	2698	0% (0/46)
	Kessentini *et al.* [24]	87% (53/61)	37 %	3156	9% (4/46)
Average (*all systems*)	NSGA-II	84%	80 %	2717	35%
	Harman *et al.* [13]	N.A	36 %	4011	4%
	Kessentini *et al.* [24]	89%	35 %	4288	9%

refactoring solutions that do not require high code changes (only 2717) comparing to other approaches having, respectively, an average of 4011 and 4288 for all studied systems. In the same time, after applying the proposed refactoring operations, we found that more than 84% of detected defects were fixed. This score is comparable to the correction score of Kessentini *et al.* (89%) that do not consider semantic preservation, neither code changes reduction nor recorded refactorings reuse (DCR is not considered in Harman *et al.* since their aim is to improve only some quality metrics). Thus, our approach performs clearly better for RP and code changes score with the cost of a slight degradation in DCR compared to Kessentini *et al.* This slight loss in the DCR is largely compensated by the significant improvement of the semantic coherence and code changes reduction. Furthermore, the corrected defects were of different types (blob, SC, and FD [3]). We found that the majority of nonfixed defects are related to the blob type. This type of defect usually requires a large number of refactoring operations and is then very difficult to correct.

To better evaluate our approach, we compare different objectives' combinations (two, three, or four objectives) to ensure the efficiency and the impact of using the four objectives we defined. To this end, we compare the refactoring results of different objectives' combinations. We also compare the results of NSGA-II with two other multiobjective algorithms (MOGA and RS) and another single-objective algorithm (GA).

To answer RQ5, we executed the NSGA-II algorithm with different combinations of objectives: maximize quality (Q), minimize semantic incoherence (S), minimize code changes (CC), and maximize the reuse of recorded refactorings (RR). Table 4.13 and Fig. 4.11 present our finding.

As illustrated in Table 4.13 and Fig. 4.11C, when the code changes' minimization objective is considered, the proposed refactoring solutions need lower code changes to be applied. Moreover, in almost all systems when recorded refactoring is combined with semantics, the RP value is

Table 4.13 Refactoring Results of Different Objectives' Combinations with NSGA-II (Average of All Systems)

Objectives Combinations	DCR (%)	RP (Empirical Evaluation) (%)	Code Changes
Q + CC	75	45	2591
Q + S	81	82	4355
Q + RC	83	54	3989
Q + S + RC	81	84	3888
Q + S + RC + CC	82	80	2717

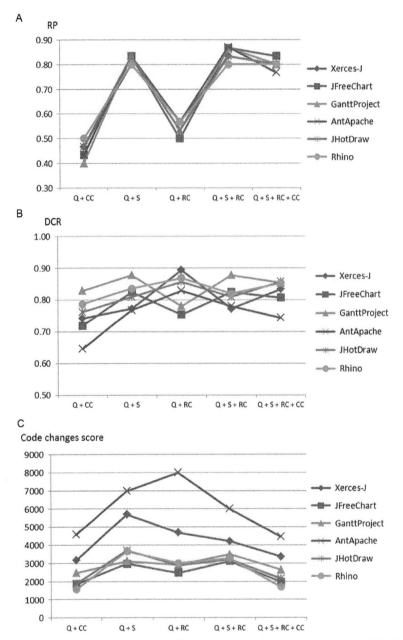

Figure 4.11 Refactoring results of different objectives' combinations with NSGA-II in terms of (A) semantic preservation, (B) defect correction ratio, and (C) code changes reduction.

improved. For example, for AntApache RP is 83% when only quality and semantics are considered; however, when recorded refactoring reuse is included, the RP is improved to 87% (Fig. 4.11A). We notice also that when code changes' reduction is included with quality, semantics, and recorded changes, the RP and DCR scores are not significantly affected. Moreover, we notice in Fig. 4.11B that there is no significant variation in terms of DCR with all different objectives' combinations. When four objectives are combined, the DCR value induces a slight degradation with an average of 82% in all systems which is even considered as promising results. Thus, the slight loss in the DCR is largely compensated by the significant improvement of the semantic coherence and code changes reduction.

Therefore, in conclusion, we found that the best compromise is obtained between the four objectives using NSGA-II comparing to the use of only two or three objectives.

To answer RQ6, we evaluate the efficiency of NSGA-II and justify the need to use multiobjective algorithms. To this end, we compared the performance of our proposal to two other multiobjective algorithms: MOGA, and a random search and a mono–objective algorithms: genetic algorithm. In a random search, the change operators (crossover and mutations) are not used, and populations are generated randomly and evaluated using the four fitness functions. In our mono–objective adaptation, we considered a single fitness function, which is the normalized average score of the four objectives using GA. Moreover, since in our NSGA-II adaptation we select a single solution without giving more importance to some objectives, we give equal weights for each fitness function value. As shown in Fig. 4.12, NSGA-II outperforms significantly comparing to MOGA, random-search, and mono-objective algorithm in terms of DCR, semantic preservation (RP), and code changes reduction. For instance, in JFreeChart, NSGA-II performs much better than MOGA, random search and GA in terms of DCR and RP scores (respectively, Fig. 4.12A and B). In addition, NSGA-II reduces significantly code changes for all studied systems, approximately to the half for Rhino (Fig. 4.12C).

Another element that should be considered when comparing the results of the four algorithms is that NSGA-II does not produce a single solution like GA, but a set of optimal solutions (nondominated solutions). The maintainer can choose a solution from them depending on his preferences in terms of compromise. However, at least for our evaluation, we need to select only one solution. To this end and in order to fully automate our

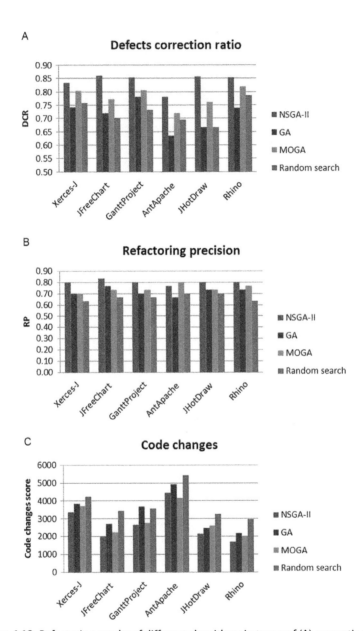

Figure 4.12 Refactoring results of different algorithms in terms of (A) semantic preservation, (B) defect correction ratio, and (C) code changes reduction.

approach, we propose to extract and suggest only one best solution from the returned set of solutions. In our case, the ideal solution has the best value of quality (equals to 1), of semantic coherence (equals to 1), and of refactoring reuse (equals to 1), and code changes (normalized value equal to 1). Hence, we select the nearest solution to the ideal one in terms of Euclidian distance.

5.4.5 Discussion

We noticed that our technique performs better than two existing approaches. We also compared different objectives' combinations and we found that the best compromise is obtained between the four objectives using NSGA-II comparing to the use of only two or three objectives. Therefore, our four objectives are efficient and complementary for providing "good" refactoring suggestion. Moreover, we found that NSGA-II performs much better than two other multiobjective algorithms: MOGA and random search, and a mono-objective algorithm: genetic algorithm.

Thus, it is important to contrast the results of multiple executions with the execution time to evaluate the performance and the stability of our approach. The execution time for finding the optimal refactoring solution with a number of iterations (stopping criteria) fixed to 6000 was less than 48 min as shown in Fig. 4.13. This indicates that our approach is reasonably scalable from the performance standpoint. Moreover, we evaluate the impact of the number of suggested refactorings on the DCR, RP, RR,

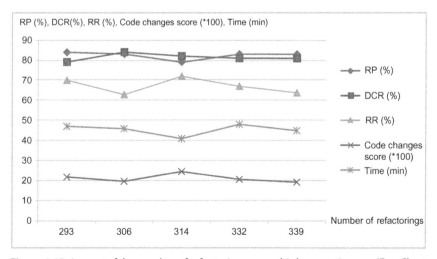

Figure 4.13 Impact of the number of refactorings on multiple executions on JFreeChart.

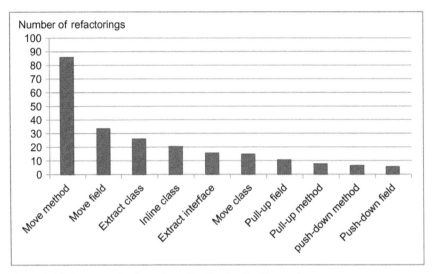

Figure 4.14 Suggested refactorings distribution for Xerces-J.

and code changes scores in five different executions. Drawn for JFreeChart, the results of Fig. 4.13 show that the number of suggested refactorings does not affect the refactoring results. Thus, a higher number of operations in a solution do not necessarily mean that the results will be better. Thus, we could conclude that our approach is scalable from the performance standpoint, especially that quality improvements are not related in general to real-time applications where time constraints are very important. In addition, the results accuracy is not affected by the number of suggested refactorings.

Another important consideration is the refactoring operations distribution. We contrast that the most suggested refactorings are move method, move field, and extract class for the vast majority of studied systems. For instance, in Xerces-J, we had different distribution of different refactoring types as illustrated in Fig. 4.14. We notice that the most suggested refactorings are related to moving code elements (fields, methods) and extract/inline class. This is mainly due to the type of defects detected in Xerces-J (most of defects are related to the blob defect) that need particular refactorings to move elements from blob class to other classes in order to reduce the number of functionalities from them. As such, refactorings like move field, move method, and extract class are likely to be more useful to correcting the blob defect. As part of future work, we plan to investigate the relationship between defect types and refactoring types.

6. CONCLUSION

In summary, the main contributions in this research work is to propose a novel approach for automating the detection and correction of design defects and to study the impact of refactoring on design defects during software evolution.

For the design defects detection step, the problem is seen as a search-based combinatorial optimization problem to find the suitable detection rules using real examples of defects. Typically, researchers and practitioners try to characterize different types of common design defects and present symptoms to search for in order to locate possible design defects in a system. In our approach, we have shown that this knowledge is not necessary to perform the detection. Instead, we use examples of design defects to generate detection rules.

After generating the detection rules, we use them in the correction step. To this end, we propose a search-based approach to find the combination of refactoring operations that best correct the detected defects. Thus, a good refactoring solution is a sequence of refactoring operations that minimize as much as possible the number of detected defects to improve software quality. This approach was tested in five open-source systems and the results are promising. In addition, we explore other objectives to optimize: (1) the number of code changes needed to apply refactorings, (2) semantic preservation, and (3) the similarity with good refactorings applied in the past to similar contexts.

To minimize the refactoring code changes, we see the refactoring process as a multiobjective optimization problem. We define a "good" refactoring solution as the combination of refactoring operations that should maximize as much as possible the number of corrected defects with minimal code modification/adaptation effort (i.e., the cost of applying the refactoring sequence). The idea is to find the best compromise between maximizing quality and minimizing code adaptability effort. In addition, we integrated the semantic preservation especially that, in our search-based approach, refactoring solutions are decided automatically. Hence, a program could be syntactically correct, have the right behavior, but model incorrectly the domain semantics. In this contribution, we propose a multiobjective optimization approach to find the best sequence of refactorings that maximize quality improvements (i.e., minimize the number of defects) and at the same time minimize potential semantic errors. Finally, to improve the automaton of refactoring, we start from the observation that recorded/historical code changes could be used to propose new refactoring solutions in similar contexts. In addition, this knowledge can be combined with structural and semantic information to improve the automation of refactoring. In this contribution, we propose a multiobjective optimization to find the compromise between all of the mentioned objectives. Our approaches were tested on a set of open-source systems and the results were promising.

As part of our future work, we are planning to investigate an empirical study to understand the correlation between correcting code smells and introducing new ones or fixing other code smells implicitly. We also plan to adapt our multiobjective approach to fix other type of defects that can occur in service-oriented architecture.

REFERENCES

[1] IEEE Std. 1219–1998, Standard for Software Maintenance, IEEE Computer Society Press, Los Alamitos, CA, 1998.
[2] A. Abran, H. Hguyenkim, Measurement of the maintenance process from a demand-based perspective, J. Softw. Maintenance Res. Pract. 5 (2) pp. 63–90 (1993).
[3] N. Fenton, S.L. Pfleeger, Software Metrics: A Rigorous and Practical Approach, second ed., International Thomson Computer Press, London, UK, 1997.
[4] M.J. Munro, Product metrics for automatic identification of "bad smell" design problems in java source-code, In: Software Metrics, 2005. 11th IEEE International Symposium, IEEE, 2005, September, pp. 15–15.
[5] S. Hassaine, F. Khomh, Y.G. Guéhéneuc, S. Hamel, IDS: an immune-inspired approach for the detection of software design smells, in: 7th International Conference on the Quality of Information and Communications Technology (QUATIC), 2010, pp. 343–348, 2010.
[6] L. Tahvildari, K. Kontogiannis, A metric-based approach to enhance design quality through meta-pattern transformation, in: Proceedings of the 7st European Conference on Software Maintenance and Reengineering , Benevento, Italy, 2003, pp. 183–192.
[7] N. Moha, Y.-G. Guéhéneuc, L. Duchien, A.-F.L. Meur, DECOR: a method for the specification and detection of code and design smells, IEEE Trans. Softw. Eng. 36 (2009) 20–36.
[8] W.J. Brown, R.C. Malveau, W.H. Brown, H.W. MCCormick III, T.J. Mowbray, Anti Patterns: Refactoring Software, Architectures, and Projects in Crisis, first ed., John Wiley and Sons, New York, USA, 1998.
[9] M. Fowler, K. Beck, J. Brant, W. Opdyke, D. Roberts, Refactoring—Improving the Design of Existing Code, first ed., Addison-Wesley, Westford, Massachusetts, USA, 1999.
[10] T. Mens, A survey of software refactoring, IEEE Trans. Softw. Eng. 30 (2) (2004) 126–139.
[11] H. Alikacem, H. Sahraoui, Détection d'anomalies utilisant un langage de description de règle de qualité, in actes du 12e colloque LMO, 2006.
[12] http://www.refactoring.com/catalog/.

[13] M. Harman, L. Tratt, Pareto optimal search based refactoring at the design level, in: Proceedings of the Genetic and Evolutionary Computation Conference (GECCO'07), 2007, pp. 1106–1113.

[14] O. Seng, J. Stammel, D. Burkhart, Search-based determination of refactorings for improving the class structure of object-oriented systems, in: Proceedings of the Genetic and Evolutionary Computation Conference (GECCO'06), 2006, pp. 1909–1916.

[15] D. Fatiregun, M. Harman, R.M. Hierons, Evolving transformation sequences using genetic algorithms, in: Proceedings of 4th SCAM, 2004, pp. 66–75.

[16] F. Qayum, R. Heckel, Local search-based refactoring as graph transformation, in: Proceedings of 1st International Symposium on Search Based Software Engineering, 2009, pp. 43–46.

[17] G. Bavota, A. De Lucia, R. Oliveto, Identifying Extract Class refactoring opportunities using structural and semantic cohesion measures, J. Syst. Softw. 84 (2011) 397–414.

[18] H. Sahraoui, R. Godin, T. Miceli, Can metrics help to bridge the gap between the improvement of OO design quality and its automation? in: Proceedings of the International Conference on Software Maintenance (ICSM'00), 2000.

[19] B. Du Bois, S. Demeyer, J. Verelst, Refactoring—improving coupling and cohesion of existing code, in: Proceedings of the 11th Working Conference on Reverse Engineering, 2004, pp. 144–151.

[20] M. O'Keeffe, M.O. Cinnéide, Search-based refactoring for software maintenance. J. Syst. Softw. 81(4) (2008) 502–516.

[21] A. Ouni, M. Kessentini, H. Sahraoui, M. Boukadoum, Maintainability defects detection and correction: a multi-objective approach, J. Autmated Softw. Eng. 20 (2013) 47–79.

[22] J.E. Gaffney, Metrics in software quality assurance, in: Proceedings of the ACM '81 Conference, ACM, New York, 1981, pp. 126–130.

[23] D.E. Goldberg, Genetic Algorithms in Search, Optimization and Machine Learning, Addison-Wesley Longman Publishing Co., Inc., Boston, MA, 1989.

[24] M. Kessentini, W. Kessentini, H. Sahraoui, M. Boukadoum, A. Ouni, Design defects detection and correction by example, in: 19th International Conference on Program Comprehension (ICPC), Kingston, Canada, 2011, pp. 81–90.

[25] A. Ouni, M. Kessentini, H. Sahraoui, M.S. Hamdi, Search-based refactoring : towards semantics preservation, in: 28th IEEE International Conference on Software Maintenance (ICSM), September 23–30, Riva del Garda, Italy, 2012.

[26] A. Ouni, M. Kessentini, H. Sahraoui, Search-based refactoring using recorded code changes, in: 17th European Conference on Software Maintenance and Reengineering (CSMR), March 5–8, Genova, Italy, 2013.

[27] G. Travassos, F. Shull, M. Fredericks, V.R. Basili, Detecting defects in object-oriented designs: using reading techniques to increase software quality, in: Proceedings of the 14th Conference on Object-Oriented Programming, Systems, Languages, and Applications, ACM Press, 1999, pp. 47–56, Denver, USA.

[28] O. Ciupke, Automatic detection of design problems in object-oriented reengineering, in: D. Firesmith (Ed.), Proceeding of 30th Conference on Technology of Object-Oriented Languages and Systems, IEEE Computer Society Press, 1999, pp. 18–32, Santa Barbara, CA, USA.

[29] R. Marinescu, Detection strategies: metrics-based rules for detecting design flaws, in: Proceedings of the 20th International Conference on Software Maintenance, IEEE Computer Society Press, 2004, pp. 350–359, Chicago Illinois, USA.

[30] M. Salehie, S. Li, L. Tahvildari, A metric-based heuristic framework to detect object-oriented design flaws, in: Proceedings of the 14th IEEE International Conference on Program Comprehension (ICPC'06), 2006.

[31] K. Erni, C. Lewerentz, Applying design metrics to object-oriented frameworks, in: Proceedings of the IEEE Symposium on Software Metrics, IEEE Computer Society Press, 1996, Berlin, Germany.

[32] F. Khomh, S. Vaucher, Y.-G. Guéhéneuc, H. Sahraoui, A Bayesian approach for the detection of code and design smells, in: Proceedings of the ICQS, 2009.

[33] C. Catal, B. Diri, Investigating the effect of dataset size, metrics sets, and feature selection techniques on software fault prediction problem, in: Information Sciences, Elsevier, vol. 179, no. 8, 2009, pp. 1040–1058.

[34] M. Kessentini, S. Vaucher, H. Sahraoui, Deviance from perfection is a better criterion than closeness to evil when identifying risky code, in: 25th IEEE/ACM International Conference on Automated Software Engineering (ASE), 2010.

[35] S.C. Kothari, L. Bishop, J. Sauceda, G. Daugherty, A pattern-based framework for software anomaly detection. Softw. Qual. J. 12 (2) (2004) 99–120.

[36] K. Dhambri, H.A. Sahraoui, P. Poulin, Visual detection of design anomalies, in: CSMR, IEEE, 2008, pp. 279–283.

[37] G. Langelier, H.A. Sahraoui, P. Poulin, visualization-based analysis of quality for large-scale software systems, in: T. Ellman, A. Zisma (Eds.), Proceedings of the 20th International Conference on Automated Software Engineering, ACM Press 2005, Long Beach, CA, USA.

[38] H. Liu, L. Yang, Z. Niu, Z. Ma, W. Shao, Facilitating software refactoring with appropriate resolution order of bad smells, in: Proceedings of the ESEC/FSE, 2009, pp. 265–268.

[39] N. Moha, A. Hacene, P. Valtchev, Y.-G. Guéhéneuc, Refactorings of design sefects using relational concept analysis, in: Raoul Medina, Sergei Obiedkov (Eds.), Proceedings of the 4th International Conference on Formal Concept Analysis (ICFCA 2008), February 2008.

[40] P. Joshi, R.K. Joshi, Concept analysis for class cohesion, in: Proceedings of the 13th European Conference on Software Maintenance and Reengineering, Kaiserslautern, Germany, 2009, pp. 237–240.

[41] Y. Kataoka, M.D. Ernst, W.G. Griswold, D. Notkin, Automated support for program refactoring using invariants, in: International Conference on Software Maintenance (ICSM), 2001, pp. 736–743.

[42] W.F. Opdyke, Refactoring: a program restructuring aid in designing object-oriented application frameworks, Ph.D. thesis, University of Illinois at Urbana-Champaign, 1992.

[43] T. Baar, S. Marković, A graphical approach to prove the semantic preservation of UML/OCL refactoring rules, In: Perspectives of Systems Informatics, Springer, Berlin Heidelberg, 2007, pp. 70–83.

[44] F. Logozzo, A. Cortesi, Semantic hierarchy refactoring by abstract interpretation, in: E.A. Emerson K.S. Namjoshi (Eds.), VMCAI 2006, LNCS 3855, 2006, pp. 313–331.

[45] D. Fatiregun, M. Harman, R. Hierons, Search-based amorphous slicing, in: InWCRE 05, Carnegie Mellon University, Pittsburgh, Pennsylvania, 2005, pp. 3–12.

[46] F.E.B. Otero, C.G. Johnson, A.A. Freitas, S.J. Thompson, Refactoring in automatically generated programs, in: International Symposium on Search Based Software Engineering, 2010.

[47] R. Davis, B. Buchanan, E.H. Shortcliffe, Production rules as a representation for a knowledge-base consultation program, Artificial Intelligence 8 (1977) 15–45.

[48] John R. Koza, Genetic Programming: On the Programming of Computers by Means of Natural Selection, MIT Press, Cambridge, MA, 1992.

[49] M. Kessentini, W. Kessentini, H. Sahraoui, M. Boukadoum, A. Ouni, Design defects detection and correction by example, 19th International Conference on Program Comprehension (ICPC), 2011, pp. 81–90.

[50] K. Deb, A. Pratap, S. Agarwal, T. Meyarivan, A fast and elitist multiobjective genetic algorithm: NSGA-II, IEEE Trans. Evol. Comput. 6 (2002) 182–197.

[51] A. Corazza, S.D. Martino, V. Maggio, LINSEN: An Efficient Approach to Split Identifiers and Expand Abbreviations, in: 28th IEEE International Conference of Software Maintenance (ICSM 2012), Riva del Garda (Trento), Italy, IEEE, 2012, pp. 233–242.

[52] R. Vallée-Rai, E. Gagnon, L.J. Hendren, P. Lam, P. Pominville, V. Sundaresan, Optimizing Java bytecode using the Soot framework: is it feasible? in: International Conference on Compiler Construction, 2000, pp. 18–34.

[53] http://www.eclipse.org/.

[54] Xerces-J. http://xerces.apache.org/xerces-j/.

[55] JFreeChart. http://www.jfree.org/jfreechart/.

[56] GanttProject. www.ganttproject.biz.

[57] AntApache. http://ant.apache.org/.

[58] JHotDraw. http://www.jhotdraw.org/.

[59] Rhino. http://www.mozilla.org/rhino/.

[60] K. Prete, N. Rachatasumrit, N. Sudan, M. Kim, Template-based reconstruction of complex refactorings, in: Proceedings of the 26th IEEE International Conference on Software Maintenance, Timisoara, Romania, IEEE CS Press, 2010, pp. 1–10.

[61] C.M. Fonseca, P.J. Fleming, Genetic algorithms for multiobjective optimization: Formulation, discussion and generalization, in: S. Forrest (Ed.), Proceedings of the Fifth International Conference on Genetic Algorithms, Morgan Kauffman, San Mateo, CA, 1993, pp. 416–423.

[62] E. Zitzler, L. Thiele, Multiobjective optimization using evolutionary algorithms—a comparative case study, in: Parallel Problem Solving from Nature, Springer, Germany, 1998, pp. 292–301.

[63] M. O'Keeffe, M.O. Cinnéide, Search-based software maintenance, in: Proceedings of the 10th European Conference on Software Maintenance and Reengineering (CSMR), 2006, pp. 249–260.

ABOUT THE AUTHORS

 **Ali Ouni** is currently a PhD student in Computer Science at the University of Montreal since 2011 under the supervision of Prof. Houari Sahraoui (University of Montreal) and Prof. Marouane Kessentini (University of Michigan). He is a member of the GEODES Software Engineering Laboratory, in the Department of Computer Science and Operational Research (DIRO), University of Montreal, Canada and a member of the SBSE Research Laboratory, University of Michigan, USA. His research interests include the application of artificial intelligence techniques to software engineering. Since 2011, he published several papers in well-ranked journals and conferences. He serves as program committee member in several conferences such as GECCO'14, CMSEBA'14, and NasBASE'15.

Marouane Kessentini is a tenure-track assistant professor at the University of Michigan. He is the founder of the research group: Search-Based Software Engineering@Michigan. He holds a Ph.D. in Computer Science, University of Montreal, Canada, 2011. His research interests include the application of artificial intelligence techniques to software engineering (search-based software engineering), software testing, model-driven engineering, software quality, and reengineering. He has published around 50 papers in conferences, workshops, books, and journals including three best paper awards. He has served as program-committee/organization member in several conferences and journals.

Houari Sahraoui is a professor of Software Engineering in the Department of Computer Science and Operations Research of the University of Montreal. He obtained his Ph.D. degree in 1995 in Computer Science, with specialization in meta-modeling and model transformation, from the Pierre & Marie Curie University, Paris. His research interests include software visualization, search-based software engineering, model transformation, and reengineering. He and his students are authors of many award-winning papers. He has been on the program, steering, or organization committees of many international, IEEE and ACM conferences, and is a member of the editorial board of three journals. He is the general chair of VISSOFT 2014.

AUTHOR INDEX

SUBJECT INDEX

CONTENTS OF VOLUMES IN THIS SERIES

Printed and bound by CPI Group (UK) Ltd, Croydon, CR0 4YY

03/10/2024

01040425-0020